NATIONAL 4 & 5

HISTORY

THE ERA OF THE GREAT WAR 1900-1928

SECOND EDITION

James McGonigle &
Claire Wood

Series Editor: John A. Kerr

AN HACHETTE UK COMPANY

The Publishers would like to thank the following for permission to reproduce copyright material:

Photo credits: p.4 Library of Congress Prints and Photographs Division; p.6 (top) Archive Farms Inc./Alamy Stock Photo, (bottom) Chronicle/Alamy Stock Photo; p.10 Robert Hunt Library/Mary Evans; p.11 (hands images on Balkans composite map) © K.-U. Häßler/ stock.adobe.com; p.12 TopFoto.co.uk p.15 TopFoto.co.uk; p.17 (bottom) David Cohen Fine Art/Mary Evans Picture Library; p.18 Punch Limited/TopFoto.co.uk; p.19 (top) Roger-Viollet/TopFoto; p.23 TopFoto.co.uk; p.24 Archivart/Alamy Stock Photo; p.25 Lordprice Collection/Alamy Stock Photo; p.27 (top) 'Will they Never Come?', recruitment poster after the Battle of Mons, 23rd August 1914 (colour litho), English Photographer, (20th century)/Private Collection/Bridgeman Images; p.34 (bottom) Library and Archives Canada item PA-149311; p.37 York Museums Trust (CC BY-SA 4.0); p.39 *The Sun*/News Syndication; p.41 TopFoto.co.uk; p.42 (top) Granger, NYC TopFoto, (bottom) TopFoto.co.uk; p.43 akg-images/Alamy Stock Photo; p.44 Mansell/Mansell/The LIFE Picture Collection/Getty Images; p.50 Ullsteinbild/TopFoto; p.52 (top) TopFoto.co.uk, (bottom) 'The Kitchen Is The Key To Victory, Eat Less Bread', 1st World War poster, c.1917 (colour litho), English School, (20th century)/Private Collection/Photo © Barbara Singer/The Bridgeman Art Library; p.54 Mitchell Library, Glasgow City Libraries and Archives via www.scran.ac.uk; p.58 Washington Imaging/Alamy Stock Photo; p.59 Woodbridge Aviation Images/Alamy Stock Photo; p.67 (left) Granger Historical Picture Archive/Alamy Stock Photo, (right) Mary Evans/Retrograph Collection; p.74 Granger, NYC/TopFoto; p.76 Suffragettes march down Princes Street, led by Flora Drummond and Emmeline Pankhurst, 1909 (b/w photo)/Edinburgh, Scotland/© Mirrorpix/Bridgeman Images; p.77 (top) Granger, NYC/TopFoto, (bottom) Mary Evans Picture Library; p.78 TopFoto.co.uk; p.79 Topham Picturepoint/TopFoto.co.uk; p.81 (top and bottom) © CSG CIC Glasgow Museums Collection; p.82 Paul Fearn/Alamy Stock Photo; p.84 © Look and Learn/Bridgeman Images; p.85 TopFoto.co.uk; p.91 © CSG CIC Glasgow Museums Collection; p.92 © Newsquest (Herald & Times). Via www.scran.ac.uk; p.96 Mary Evans Picture Library/Onslow Auctions Limited; p.97 (top) Granger, NYC/TopFoto; (bottom) Wikipedia.

Acknowledgements: p.5 extract from *Bright RED Study Guide: N5 History – Scotland* by Chris & Aileen MacKay (Bright Red Publishing, 2013). Reproduced by permission of Bright Red Publishing; p.8 extract from *Scotland in the Twentieth Century* by Tom Devine and Richard Finlay (Edinburgh University Press, 1996); p.26 letter to *The Nation* on 15 August 1914 by Bertrand Russell. Reproduced by permission of The Bertrand Russell Peace Foundation Ltd.; p.33 extract from 'The Realities of War' by R.A. Scott Macfie from *The Imperial War Museum Book of the First World War: A Great Conflict Recalled in Previously Unpublished Letters, Diaries, Documents and Memoirs*. Reproduced with permission of Pan Macmillan through PLSclear; p.38 statistics from *General Annual Report of the British Army 1913–1919*, pp 1921, xx, Cmd 1193; H. Newbolt, *History of the Great War. Naval Operations* (1931), vol. v, Appendix J; A. Jones, *History of the Great War. War in the Air* (1937), Appendices 35–6.; p.38 extract from Piper Daniel Laidlaw recorded in *The Gazette (London Gazette)*, issue 29371, page 11447, 18 November 1915; pp.39, 52, 69 & 93 extracts from *The Flowers of the Forest* by Trevor Royle. Copyright © Trevor Royle 2006. Reproduced with permission of Birlinn Limited through PLSclear; pp.53–4 extract from *Little Grey Partridge: First World War Diary of Ishobel Ross Who Served with the Scottish Women's Hospitals Unit in Serbia* by Ishobel Ross (Aberdeen University Press, 1988); p.54 extract from *The Private Papers of Miss M. Chisholm* © IWM; p.55 extract from *Blighty: British society in the era of the Great War* by Gerard De Groot (Longman, 1996). Reproduced by permission of Gerard De Groot; p.56 extract from War Office: *Soldiers Died in the Great War 1914–1919* (War Office, London, 1921): Part 6 The Royal Scots (Lothian Regiment), Part 46 The Black Watch (Royal Highlanders), Part 63 The Highland Light Infantry, Part 65 The Gordon Highlanders. Contains public sector information licensed under the Open Government Licence v3.0; p.61 extract from *Scottish Popular Politics: From Radicalism to Labour* by W. Hamish Fraser (Edinburgh University Press, 2000); p.73 extract from *The Hidden History of Glasgow's Women: The THENEW Factor* by Elspeth King (Mainstream Publishing, 1993).

Every effort has been made to trace all copyright holders, but if any have been inadvertently overlooked the Publishers will be pleased to make the necessary arrangements at the first opportunity.

Although every effort has been made to ensure that website addresses are correct at time of going to press, Hodder Gibson cannot be held responsible for the content of any website mentioned in this book. It is sometimes possible to find a relocated web page by typing in the address of the home page for a website in the URL window of your browser.

Hachette UK's policy is to use papers that are natural, renewable and recyclable products and made from wood grown in sustainable forests. The logging and manufacturing processes are expected to conform to the environmental regulations of the country of origin.

Orders: please contact Bookpoint Ltd, 130 Park Drive, Milton Park, Abingdon, Oxon OX14 4SE.
Telephone: (44) 01235 827827. Fax: (44) 01235 400454. Lines are open 9.00–5.00, Monday to Saturday, with a 24-hour message answering service. Visit our website at www.hoddereducation.co.uk.
Hodder Gibson can be contacted directly at hoddergibson@hodder.co.uk

Impression number	5	4	3	2	1
Year	2022	2021	2020	2019	2018

Cover photo © Peredniankina/123RF.com
Illustrations by Gray Publishing
Produced and typeset in 11/11.5pt Folio Light by Integra Software Services Pvt. Ltd., Pondicherry, India
Printed in Slovenia

A catalogue record for this title is available from the British Library

ISBN: 978 1 5104 2932 1

Contents

Preface   iv

The Assignment: what you need to know   v

  1   Introduction   1

  2   What was Scotland like in 1900?   2

Section 1   Scots on the Western Front

  3   Why did war break out in 1914?   9

  4   What happened in Europe by the end of 1914?   21

  5   What was it like for Scots fighting on the Western Front?   32

Section 2   Domestic impact of war: society and culture

  6   How did the war affect people back at home?   48

Section 3   Domestic impact of war: industry and economy

  7   What impact did the war have on Scotland's industry and economy?   62

Section 4   Domestic impact of war: politics

  8   What effects did the war have on the role of women?   72

  9   What impact did the war have on politics in Scotland?   89

10   To what extent had Scotland changed by 1928?   95

Glossary   101

Index   104

Preface

This is one of a series of six titles fully updated for the National 4 & 5 History courses to be assessed from 2018 onwards. Students should study three main sections in National 4 & 5 History, with a very wide selection of topics to choose from (five in the first two, ten in the third). This series covers two topics in each section.

The six titles in the series are:

▶ National 4 & 5 History: Migration and Empire 1830–1939
▶ National 4 & 5 History: The Era of the Great War 1900–1928
▶ National 4 & 5 History: The Atlantic Slave Trade 1770–1807
▶ National 4 & 5 History: Changing Britain 1760–1914
▶ National 4 & 5 History: Hitler and Nazi Germany 1919–1939
▶ National 4 & 5 History: Free at Last? Civil Rights in the USA 1918–1968

Each book will contain comprehensive coverage of the four SQA key issue areas for National 5, as well as guidance and practice on Assignment writing and assessment procedures.

The Assignment: what you need to know

National 5

What is the Assignment for National 5?

The Assignment is written under exam conditions and then sent to the SQA to be marked. It counts for 20 marks out of a total of 100, so doing well in the Assignment can provide you with a very useful launchpad for overall success in the National 5 exam.

The assignment has two stages:

▶ research (the gathering together of your findings and sources). This can be done at any appropriate point in the course.
▶ production of evidence (the writing up, in exam conditions, in the allotted one-hour sitting).

How should I write my Assignment?

You are given marks for showing certain skills in your Assignment. Firstly, you *must* choose a question to write about. That means your title should end with a question mark. Once your question is sorted, you must aim to:

▶ Write an introduction that sets the context for your question and which outlines different, relevant factors.
▶ Organise your information so that it makes sense as a balanced answer to your main question.
▶ Use your own knowledge and understanding to explain and analyse the question you have chosen.
▶ Use information gathered from *at least* two relevant sources to address and support these factors. For example, two books or one book plus an interview.
▶ Use other detailed information to support these.
▶ Evaluate which of the factors were more important than others.
▶ Identify and assess different perspectives and/or points of view (try to include *at least* two).
▶ Reach a conclusion that states what you think is the main answer to your question.
▶ Give reasons to support your conclusion.

What should I write about?

Here are some suggestions for suitable questions based on the content of this book:

✓ How important was the Scottish martial tradition as a reason for high levels of voluntary recruitment at the outbreak of war in 1914–15?
✓ To what extent was Haig's leadership the reason for the lack of success at the Battle of Loos?
✓ How important were jute and textiles to Scotland's war effort during the First World War?
✓ To what extent was the First World War the main reason for women gaining the vote in 1918?
✓ To what extent was conscientious objection to the First World War the result of religious views?

The following list contains examples of badly worded Assignment titles:

✕ The fighting of Scots on the Western Front.
✕ Effects of the First World War on Scottish industry.
✕ The effects of the First World War on Scottish culture.
✕ Changes to the Scottish economy during the First World War.
✕ Effects of the First World War on the Labour Party.

These are just headings. You must have a question so that you can answer it. The bad choices would result in telling a story.

Be safe! There are no prizes for giving yourself a difficult question that you have made up yourself. Choose something from the history you have already been studying. You could choose a title from a past exam paper: www.sqa.org.uk/sqa/47447 or modify a past-paper question, with help from your teacher.

Avoid doing something risky – you only get one chance at this Assignment.

How long should my Assignment be?

Your Assignment has no word count limit – it all depends on how much you can write in the permitted hour. Most Assignments are about four or five pages long.

Remember that you also have a Resource Sheet to help you

On your Resource Sheet you will write out the sources that you will refer to in your essay. This will show the marker that you have researched, selected and organised your information.

Your Resource Sheet will be sent to the SQA with your finished Assignment. You will not be given a mark for your completed Resource Sheet, but markers will use it to see that you have done the necessary research and have found appropriate sources to use in your Assignment. The Resource Sheet is *yours*. You can change it, colour it or print it out. You can write it anywhere, anytime before you write your Assignment under exam conditions. You can include bullet points, spidergrams (spider diagrams), notes, names, dates. The only strict rules are that your Resource Sheet must:

▶ not be longer than 200 words
▶ be on one side of A4
▶ contain the title and author of *at least* two sources you are referring to in your Assignment.

You must **not** copy out large sections from your resource page into your Assignment, but you **can** copy across quotes from your sources that you have in your Resource Sheet.

National 4: Added Value Unit

The Assignment (sometimes called the Added Value Unit) lets you show off your skills as you research a historical issue. You have a lot of choice in what you can investigate and you can also choose to present your findings in different ways. That means you don't *have* to write an essay to display your skills, knowledge and understanding.

To be successful in National 4 you have to show you can research and use information by doing the following things:

▶ Choosing an appropriate historical theme or event for study. Your teacher can help you choose.
▶ Collecting relevant evidence from *at least* two sources of information.
▶ Organising and using the information that you have collected to help you write about the subject you have chosen.
▶ Describing what your chosen subject is about.
▶ Explaining why your chosen subject happened (its cause) or explaining what happened next because of your chosen subject (its effects).

As you work through this book you will give presentations, and create posters, diagrams and artwork. All these things could be part of your National 4 Assignment. You then have to present your findings.

Don't worry – if you get stuck your teacher is allowed to give you help and advice at *any* stage as you do your Assignment.

Do I have to write a long essay?

No, you don't. You can choose how you present your Assignment at National 4. For example, you could give a talk and then be asked some questions about your subject by your teacher. You could do a PowerPoint presentation or keep a learning log. You might decide to design a poster or use some other way to display your work. But yes, you *could* write an essay if you wanted to!

1 Introduction

What is this course about?

This book is about the experiences of Scots in the Great War and the impact of the war on life in Scotland. The Great War is also known as the First World War.

The book examines the impact of technology on the soldiers on the Western Front. It also considers how life changed for people at home and how the war began to affect them.

What will this book help me to do?

This book will help you to be successful in your National 4 and 5 History course. It contains everything you need to know about all the key issues and descriptions of content provided by the SQA for 'The Era of the Great War 1900–1928'.

The book provides advice and examples to help you to answer all the different types of questions you are likely to face in the National 5 exam.

Finally, this book will provide guidance to help you to work on the Added Value Assignment tasks.

2 What was Scotland like in 1900?

What is this chapter about?

In 1900, Britain was the world's greatest power. It ruled an empire which covered a quarter of the world's surface and Scotland played an important part in this. As the 'second city of the empire', Glasgow was very significant. Its success and wealth had been built on heavy industries such as shipbuilding and steel making. However, there were problems emerging that were starting to threaten Glasgow's – and Scotland's – industrial success.

Glasgow's key industries were growing old and facing new competition from other countries which were catching up fast.

There was unrest among the industrial workers who wanted better pay and conditions. In political terms, the Scottish Labour Party was beginning to attract support from the industrial classes. There was also a demand for better housing, health care and educational opportunities.

Despite appearances, Glasgow, Scotland and Britain were facing challenges that would lead to trouble in the future.

By the end of this chapter you should be able to:

▶ Describe what it was like to live and work in Scotland in 1900.
▶ Describe the problems facing people living in Glasgow.
▶ Explain the problems and difficulties affecting the Scottish economy.

The British Empire

When George V came to the throne in 1910, Britain was the world's greatest power. Not only was George the king of Great Britain, he was also Emperor of India and his government ruled an **empire** that covered 25 per cent of the world.

> ## GLOSSARY
> **Empire** a group of nations under the control of a single ruling power

A young person leaving Glasgow in 1900 could go around the world and never need to travel through a 'foreign' country. Sailing west from Glasgow on a British-built and registered ship, Canada was the first landfall. From there the journey would take the traveller south to British Honduras and then further south to the Falkland Islands. East from the Falklands would see our visitor enter South Africa. Further east would be Australia and then New Zealand. Moving north, the delights of Hong Kong and then Singapore were to be enjoyed before calling in on the 'jewel of the empire' – India. From here it was a long voyage across the Red Sea and through the British-controlled Suez Canal, then home via Cyprus, Malta, Gibraltar and back to Glasgow. It would seem that there was never a truer saying than 'the sun never set on the British Empire'.

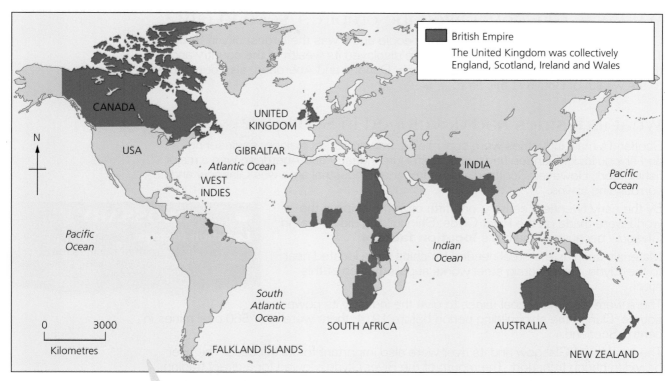

The British Empire in 1900

Use Google Earth™ to follow the exact route around the world described on page 2.

Activity 1

Research

Search the internet to find a detailed map of the British Empire in 1914 and answer the following questions.

1 Which was the smallest territory in the empire? Which was the biggest? Which was furthest away from Britain? Which was nearest to Britain?
2 Use the information you find to explain the meaning of the saying, 'the sun never set on the British Empire'.

Why was Glasgow called the empire's 'second city'?

Glasgow's population was over a million people and it was the largest city in Scotland. The new City Chambers in George Square displayed its wealth to the country and to the world. Scotland's other cities, Edinburgh, Dundee and Aberdeen, also contributed to the wealth of Britain at this time.

What industries had developed in Scotland?

Scotland's main industries were coal mining, iron and steel making, engineering and shipbuilding. Dundee had a successful jute industry and Aberdeen was a major fishing port. However, Scotland's most important industrial area was Glasgow and its surrounding towns.

By the early twentieth century, one-fifth of all the ships in the world were made on the River Clyde. Shipbuilding did so well in Glasgow because of the city's **location factors**.

Materials such as the steel needed for ships were located near to the Clyde. Ravenscraig steel works supplied much of this steel.

> ### GLOSSARY
> **Location factors** reasons why companies set up their businesses where they do

There were also many coal mines to give the industry its power source. During the shipbuilding period before 1914, there were over 560 coal mines in central Scotland.

The location of Glasgow and its river were also important for its success. The river provided cheap transport. The mouth of the River Clyde allowed for a direct trading route between Scotland and the rest of the world. This encouraged more industry to locate in the Glasgow area.

Shipbuilding and engineering companies such as John Brown, Beardmore and Napier were world leaders in these industries and provided employment for hundreds of thousands of workers. At the start of the pre-war period, Glasgow and the west of Scotland seemed to have a secure industrial outlook.

Glasgow City Chambers at the start of the twentieth century

> Use the internet to find a large picture of this building and others in the Merchant City part of Glasgow. Examine the architecture. What is it about the late Victorian buildings that suggests power and wealth and pride?

What problems did the Scottish economy face?

In the 1900s, industry started to struggle. Some of the reasons were that raw materials, such as coal, were running out. There was also competition from other countries. Foreign workers would work for less money. This meant that foreign goods were cheaper than those made in Britain.

Why was there industrial unrest?

A modern historian writing in 2013 describes industrial unrest in Scotland:

Strikes *over pay and conditions were common in Scotland. In March 1911, the 10,000 employees of the Singer factory in Clydebank went on strike over changes to their working conditions. Throughout 1910–14 a number of strikes broke out across Scotland and Britain. The strikes often resulted in scenes of violence which led to the government taking strong action. During strikes in Dundee in December 1911, extra police and soldiers from the Black Watch had to be sent in to keep order. In March 1913, another strike in the city saw 30,000 millworkers stop work. Later that year, a strike at Leith docks worried the local council. An attempt was made by some of the strikers to blow up one of the walls of the docks.*

> **GLOSSARY**
>
> **Strikes** withdrawal of work to get employers to give in to workers' demands
>
> **Trade unions** associations representing particular groups of workers

British industry was facing a period of industrial unrest. Strike action was the most common way to force employers to give the workers what they wanted. **Trade unions** would ask for better pay and conditions, and would threaten to go on strike if their demands were not met. These demands were made to help their members to meet the rising cost of living. In 1912, wages in Scotland's cities were ten per cent lower than in English cities while living costs (food and rent) were five per cent higher. Most employers were unwilling to give in to such demands and industrial unrest followed.

Which political parties controlled Scotland?

The two main parties at this time were the Liberals, led by Prime Minister Herbert Asquith, and the Conservatives, led by Arthur Balfour. In Scotland, socialist parties also developed. In 1900, the Scottish Trade Unions and the Independent Labour Party (ILP) helped to create a new political party for the working classes. It was called the Labour Representation Committee, or the Labour Party for short.

However, by the end of 1910, the Liberal Party was the biggest force in Scottish politics, as the results from the general elections in the table show.

Year	Liberals	Labour	Conservatives
1906	58	2	10
Jan. 1910	58	3	9
Dec. 1910	58	3	9

Number of seats in parliament for Scottish Members of Parliament

> Use the figures in the table to prove the claim that Scotland was controlled by two political parties.

What problems did the Scottish people face?

In the nineteenth century, Scotland's population had grown rapidly. Scotland's four cities contained about 30 per cent of the total Scottish population. By 1900, many houses were no longer fit for purpose and had become **slums**.

An investigation into housing conditions in Scotland in 1911 found that 13 per cent of the population lived in overcrowded conditions. The typical home was a tenement flat which was dark, gloomy and insanitary. Many families shared just one toilet among them. The smell was appalling. In these dirty conditions, disease spread rapidly and people did not live for very long. This same investigation found that one in every ten Scottish homes only had a single room.

GLOSSARY

Slums homes unfit for people to live in

Crofters tenant farmers in the Highlands of Scotland

Describe the condition of the buildings. Explain why life would be hard for people living in these conditions.

136 Saltmarket, Glasgow, around 1900

Why was there unrest in the Highlands?

In the Highlands, the most urgent issue was that of land to live on and to farm. The **Crofters'** Holdings Act of 1886 gave people renting land and housing in the Highlands some protection from being thrown off their farms. However, these Highland tenants were still evicted from their crofts before the war and this problem continued after the war.

Make up a list of adjectives to describe what you see in the photo.

Highland crofters in 1886

Activity 2

Summarise this chapter

▶ Put the heading 'What was Scotland like in 1914?' in your workbook or work file.
▶ Draw a table like the one below.
▶ Find at least two pieces of information to describe each part of Scottish society.

	Evidence about Scotland before 1914
Scotland's people	
Scotland's industry and economy	
Problems facing Scotland	
Scotland's political parties	

Activity 3

Design a presentation

Create a visual presentation on the question: 'What was Scotland like before the First World War?'

Work in small groups or pairs and create a presentation that will last no more than four minutes. Your presentation must contain visual material; PowerPoint is just one of the possibilities.

You should each identify a piece of information that you think best explains what Scotland was like before the First World War and be prepared to explain your choice.

Question practice

National 4

Source A is by a modern historian.

SOURCE A

Scotland was changing before 1914. It had a lot of immigration and most people had moved to live in the towns. Scotland was also developing its industry with strengths in engineering and shipbuilding. However, Scotland remained proud of its military tradition.

Describe what Scotland was like before 1914. You should use Source A and your own knowledge.

Success criteria

Include at least two points or one developed piece of information on what Scotland was like before 1914.

National 5

1 Describe the changes in Scottish society before 1914. (4 marks)

Here are some hints to get you started:

- Describe the effects of the successes and issues facing industry in Scotland.
- Describe how Scotland's changing economy affected Scottish people before 1914.
- Describe the industrial unrest in Scotland.
- Describe what Scottish politics was like before 1914 and how it was changing.
- Describe the social issues in Scotland caused by industrialisation and people moving to towns.

Success criteria

- You will need to write an introduction sentence that gives a judgement on the question. For example, 'There were many changes in Scottish society before 1914.'
- Four marks are given for four properly described points about four different things.
- You can also get 4 marks for giving your answer in developed points: describing a point, then developing this point with additional detail in a separate sentence. This can reduce the amount you have to write. You will need to give two developed points for a 4-mark answer.
- Do not list your points together; you will only get 1 mark for this. You need four different sentences.

Source A is about what Scotland was like before 1914. It is by Tom Devine and Richard Finlay, both modern historians.

SOURCE A

At the beginning of the twentieth century, Scotland by any measure was one of the great manufacturing centres of the world. The Clyde built nearly a fifth of the world's total output of ships. In the Western lowlands, the coal, engineering and shipbuilding and metal manufacturers sent products to all parts of the globe. The great fact of Scottish industry in the twentieth century was how that industry declined.

2 Evaluate the usefulness of Source A as evidence of what Scotland was like before 1914. (You may want to comment on what type of source it is, who wrote it, when they wrote it, why they wrote it, what they say and what has been missed out.) (5 marks)

Success criteria

- You will need to write an introduction sentence that gives a judgement on the question. For example, 'Source A is quite/very useful as evidence of …'
- For every point, you must say whether it makes the source *more* or *less* useful. If you don't do this, you will not get the mark.
- Up to 4 marks are given for evaluative comments about the author, type, purpose and timing of the source.
- Up to 2 marks are given for evaluative comments on the relevant parts of the source content that you select.
- Up to 2 marks are given for evaluative comments relating to points of information missing from the source.

3 Why did war break out in 1914?

What is this chapter about?

Before 1914, tension was increasing among the Great Powers. The Great Powers were the major states of Europe, such as Britain, Russia, Germany, France and Austria–Hungary. There were a number of reasons for this tension. Some of the reasons were long term, such as rivalry over trade and empire, and some were short term, such as the naval arms race. The assassination of the heir to the throne of the Austro-Hungarian Empire led to these states becoming involved in a European war. Britain joined this conflict on 4 August 1914.

By the end of this chapter you should be able to:

▶ Explain why there was tension among the leading European powers by 1914.
▶ Describe the reasons for war breaking out in 1914.

Why do countries go to war?

In the years since the end of the Second World War in 1945, there have been over 300 separate wars around the globe. Just like people, nations see things that make them angry, worried or jealous. Usually, an argument begins and then that can become violent and lead to fighting. This was the situation in Europe by 1914. There was a great deal of fear and suspicion. The murder of the Austrian archduke in the summer of 1914 was an example of this. His death had a 'snowball' effect that led to war among most European nations only a few weeks later. How did this happen? Historians have been puzzling over this ever since.

Why was there rivalry between empires?

By 1914, many European nations had large empires. Colonies were important because:

▶ they provided food and raw materials
▶ they were a market for investment and industrial products of the mother country
▶ they provided soldiers in times of war
▶ they had a strategic position which allowed the mother country to protect its interests abroad.

Germany was very jealous of Britain and France because they had very large empires. By contrast, the German Empire was not large at all. Germany had only become a single, united country in 1871. By this time much of the world had already been divided up. The ruler of Germany, Kaiser Wilhelm II, wanted Germany to have more colonies to make it as important as Britain and France. From Britain's point of view, the Kaiser's ambition was worrying.

L'INGORDO
TROP DUR

Describe in detail what you can see. What does this show about how people thought about the Kaiser? Sketch a similar cartoon from a German point of view, showing a more positive impression of German empire building. Think about the symbolism of what you draw.

A 1915 cartoon showing the ambitions of the Kaiser. The words mean 'The glutton – too hard.'

Why was there rivalry over trade?

All countries wanted to be independent when it came to vital supplies. New markets were always needed for the products from the ruling country's industries. European countries guarded their empires jealously and were suspicious of any new countries, such as Germany, trying to increase their influence. Mother countries were trying to make money from developing their colonies. Rivalry over world trade was another cause of pre-war tension.

What was the effect of Pan-Slavism?

In the Austro-Hungarian Empire, many millions of Czechs, Slovaks and Croats wanted the freedom to speak their own language and to practise their own customs. These 'minority ethnic groups' hated their rulers and wanted **Pan-Slavism**. Most of these peoples were **Slavic** in origin. They looked to the largest Slav state, Russia, to help protect them from their 'foreign' rulers. However, this was regarded as interference by states such as Austria–Hungary, which wanted to control the Slavic people in its own empire without interference from any other country.

> **GLOSSARY**
>
> **Pan-Slavism** a movement trying to bring about the unity of all Slav nations
>
> **Slavic** a group of people found in central and eastern Europe

Competing ambitions in the Balkans

> How does this image show how tension in the Balkans could explode into a much larger conflict? Is this an effective summary of Balkan tensions before 1914? How would you improve it?

Activity 1

Get your own copy of a map of Europe. Using your own research on Google Maps™, colour it in using different pencils to indicate Russia, Austria–Hungary, Germany and the Balkans.

▶ Using the map, the cartoon sketch you did earlier and the information you have read, explain why the Balkans were a source of conflict before 1914. You should refer to:
  ▶ rivalry over trade
  ▶ Pan-slavism
  ▶ rivalry over control of the Balkans.
▶ Describe how a problem in the Balkans could help lead to the outbreak of a European war.

Activity 2

Analysing a cartoon

Look at the 'Balkan Troubles' cartoon below and answer the following questions.

THE BOILING POINT.

▶ Describe in detail what you see happening in the cartoon.
▶ Which European countries do the figures on top of the pot represent?
▶ If this was a real picture, why would the people on the pot look worried?
▶ This cartoon is not a real picture but represents the problems affecting Europe
  in 1914. Using all your available information, explain in detail all the problems shown
  by the cartoon.

These issues could well be described as long-term causes of the First World War.

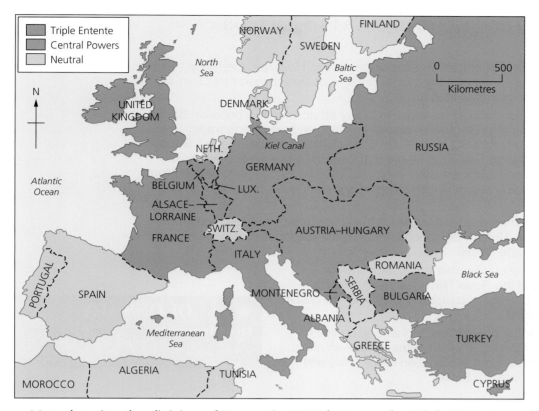

Triple Entente
Central Powers
Neutral

Map showing the division of Europe in 1914 between the Triple Entente *and the* Central Powers

What were the short-term causes of the war?

Why did Alsace–Lorraine cause problems between France and Germany?

France and Germany did not like each other. Why was that? In 1871, Germany defeated France in a war. At the end of the war, Germany took control of two eastern parts of France: Alsace and Lorraine.

Alsace and Lorraine were rich in raw materials and their loss was a blow to the French economy, as well as to French pride. France was determined to regain these areas, even if it meant war, and this tension between France and Germany over Alsace and Lorraine was another cause of the First World War.

The provinces of Alsace and Lorraine

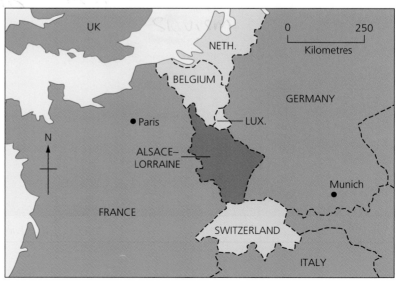

13

Why did Britain and Germany not like each other by 1914?

Britain had the world's largest empire and the biggest navy. However, Germany wanted to be the strongest nation in the world. Britain was determined that Germany would not become more powerful than it.

Britain believed that its navy should be larger than any other country's because Britain needed such a large fleet to protect its overseas colonies and worldwide trade. Germany also wanted to build a big navy. In 1895, the Kiel Canal was opened, linking the Baltic Sea with the North Sea. That meant that German ships could leave their bases in the Baltic Sea and quickly reach the North Sea. The British were worried that the Germans could possibly attack British shipping and then escape quickly back to port through the canal.

Britain was even more worried when German Admiral von Tirpitz ordered many more warships to be built after 1898. Many people thought the reason for having such a large fleet was to challenge Britain.

In response to the supposed German threat, Admiral Sir John Fisher modernised the Royal Navy. His most important improvement was the building of a brand new type of battleship called the **Dreadnought**.

Dreadnoughts were faster, could travel further and could hit targets from a greater distance than any other ship then afloat. They were also more heavily protected than other ships and could survive being damaged in battle.

> **GLOSSARY**
>
> **Dreadnought** a new class of super-battleship

The location of the Kiel Canal in Germany

> Why do you think the opening of the Kiel Canal made Britain more suspicious of Germany? (Hint: Germany's navy could hide in the Baltic Sea. It was difficult for Germany's enemies to get there.)

What effect did this new ship have on all other naval ships at this time?

HMS Dreadnought – *the first of the Dreadnoughts*

Germany soon developed its own super-battleships. The two countries were now in a race to see who could build the most. By 1914, Britain possessed 29 to the 17 built by Germany. This race soured relations between Britain and Germany and contributed to increased tension before 1914.

Activity 3

Summarise this chapter

This task is to help you to summarise the information in this chapter so far. Below is a summary paragraph. In it, the key words have been turned into ANAGRAMS. You need to unscramble the anagrams and copy the paragraph into your workbook or work file.

There were many causes of the First World War. There was rivalry between **NBRAITI, CEFNRA** and **YERGMAN** over land. They were also rivals over **DRAET**. There were also nationalist movements like **NAP MIVSLAS** which wanted independence for their peoples. France wanted revenge for Germany taking **SCEALA OLRRNEAI** from them. Germany and Britain also became rivals in the **LNAVA MARS EARC**.

Activity 4

Create an art spiral

Your teacher will place a large spiral of paper in the centre of an open space. The paper should be large enough to allow for easy movement and space for contributions from the whole class.

Work in pairs. Each pair should choose a free space on the spiral and draw something that represents a main cause of tension between the Great Powers. The drawing should be backed up by a short explanation of what the picture represents. Each explanation should contain two reasons why the cause being drawn increased tension between the Great Powers.

After a length of time decided by your teacher, move on to another free area of the spiral and draw a picture of another main cause of the war. This should continue until all space on the spiral is filled up.

Once finished, the class will look at the whole spiral and evaluate contributions from each pair. Pairs might be asked to explain or develop their contribution.

Activity 5

Work in pairs or small groups. Put the heading 'Causes of tension between the Great Powers' on a piece of paper and draw a table beneath with two columns. In the first column, write down all the causes of tension between the Great Powers. In the second column, put the heading 'Risk rating'.

Give each cause of tension a mark out of ten, depending on how important you think it is as a reason for a possible war. A mark of one would be unlikely to cause war; a mark of ten would be almost certain to result in war. Make sure that all the causes of tension between the Great Powers are given a risk rating.

Debate the relative importance of each cause of tension in your class.

Why did Europe become divided into two rival camps?

The Great Powers began to look for other countries that might help them in a time of war. Countries that help each other are called allies.

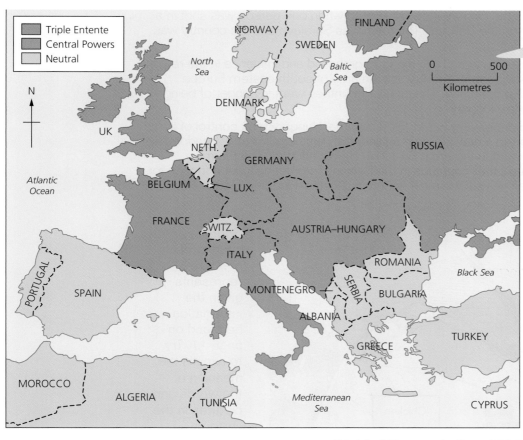

Divided Europe before 1914

In the years before 1914, Europe was described as 'two armed camps'. Looking at the map, why do you think Germany, Austria–Hungary and Italy were called the Central Powers? Why was Germany worried about the alliance between France and Russia?

A Sutherland china cream jug which includes the shields of the Triple Entente and the flags of their allies

Through research, identify the countries, other than those of the Triple Entente, whose flags are shown. Write a brief account of how you carried out this task.

Why was there trouble in the Balkans?

Why were the Balkans important as a cause of the First World War?

The answer is because the First World War started when one person was shot in a town in a small country in the Balkans. The town was Sarajevo and the country was Bosnia.

Austria–Hungary and Russia were both trying to grab land and influence in the region. The Balkan region is not just one country; it is an area of south-eastern Europe containing lots of smaller countries. The smaller countries were in danger of being swallowed up by Austria–Hungary.

Bosnia wanted to be independent but in 1908, Austria–Hungary took control of it. The Bosnians now started a new struggle against the Austrians for their freedom. This led to a series of wars in the area. By 1914, Serbia had become the main supporter of Bosnia and other countries in the Balkans, promoting independence for the Balkans, and therefore was the main enemy of Austria–Hungary. Serbia also had a big friend – Russia!

Suggest which country each creature represents given the information here and on page 11. Try to explain the meaning of the words and pictures in the cartoon.

Bear

Chicken

Double-headed eagle

THE POWER BEHIND.

AUSTRIA (*at the ultimatum stage*). "I DON'T QUITE LIKE HIS ATTITUDE. SOMEBODY MUST BE BACKING HIM."

A cartoon published in the British magazine Punch in 1914

What happened at Sarajevo on 28 June 1914?

The heir to the throne of the Austro-Hungarian Empire was called Archduke Franz Ferdinand. He and his wife planned to visit Sarajevo, the Bosnian capital, on 28 June 1914. Meanwhile, Bosnian terrorists, backed by the Serbian secret police, had made a plan to assassinate the royal couple.

Historians now think that Austrian politicians knew about the assassination plot but allowed the visit to go ahead because the murder of the archduke would give Austria an excuse to blame Serbia. The scene was set for the murder of one man and his wife to start a chain reaction that would lead to the deaths of nearly ten million people by the end of 1918.

'Assassination has never changed the history of the world.' Do you agree with this statement? Now think again. Did the assassination really change what was likely to happen anyway?

A newspaper's drawing of Franz Ferdinand's assassination in 1914

Summary of what led to the First World War

There were both long- and short-term reasons why Europe went to war in 1914.

Long-term		Short-term
Empire rivalry		Alsace and Lorraine
Trade rivalry		Naval arms race
Pan-Slavism		Alliances
		Trouble in the Balkans

The spark that ignited all of these was the assassination at Sarajevo on 28 June 1914.

Activity 6

'Walk around, talk around'

Work in pairs or in small groups. Take a large piece of paper and draw a triangle that fills most of the page.

Your teacher will allocate a period of time. Fill the triangle with as much information as you can on the short- and long-term causes of the First World War. Once your time is up, leave your paper and move on to the next group's paper.

Your teacher will allocate another period of time. Add more information to the new group's paper outside the triangle. Keep moving round until all the information is on the paper or the paper is filled.

As a class, discuss and confirm that all main causes of the First World War have been included on each group's paper.

All of the class should take part in discussing and recording information.

Activity 7

Use a full page in your workbook or work file and write the question 'What were the main causes of the First World War?' as a heading.

Draw up a table with two columns: one titled 'Cause of the war' and the other 'Evidence'. Write down the long- and short-term causes of the war in the 'Cause of the war' column.

Add at least two pieces of information from the textbook to explain how each was a cause of the First World War under the 'Evidence' column.

Be prepared to explain your answers.

4 What happened in Europe by the end of 1914?

What is this chapter about?

From 28 June until 4 August 1914, the European nations gradually found themselves at war with each other. In all of the countries involved, there was an outpouring of nationalist feeling and men rushed to join their armed forces. The opening battles were fought to try to stop the Germans from capturing large areas of north-eastern France after they had invaded Belgium. This invasion prompted Britain to declare war on Germany. Germany faced enemy countries on two fronts, France in the west and Russia in the east, and came up with the Schlieffen Plan. The failure of the Schlieffen Plan after the Battle of the Marne meant that war became static. As a result, the war of movement became one of stalemate and trench warfare.

By the end of this chapter you should be able to:

‣ Describe the timescale for the outbreak of war.
‣ Describe what happened in the opening months of the war.
‣ Explain why Scots rushed to join the armed forces.

Summer 1914

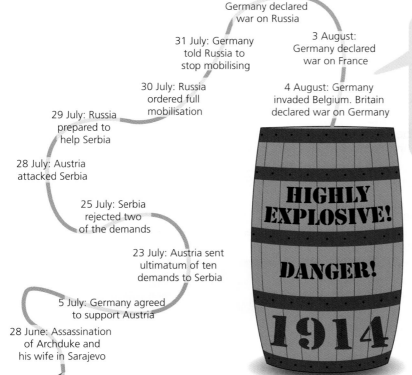

1 August: Germany declared war on Russia

31 July: Germany told Russia to stop mobilising

3 August: Germany declared war on France

30 July: Russia ordered full mobilisation

4 August: Germany invaded Belgium. Britain declared war on Germany

29 July: Russia prepared to help Serbia

28 July: Austria attacked Serbia

25 July: Serbia rejected two of the demands

23 July: Austria sent ultimatum of ten demands to Serbia

5 July: Germany agreed to support Austria

28 June: Assassination of Archduke and his wife in Sarajevo

HIGHLY EXPLOSIVE!

DANGER!

1914

Make a diagram, display or flowchart that uses this information to show how Europe rushed towards war in 1914. One idea would be to draw a staircase going down. On each step you present clearly what happened that took Europe one step closer to war.

A timeline of events

This cartoon shows similar information to the timeline on page 21. It shows how a local war expanded into a European war.

'A Chain of Friendship.' This is a modern redrawing of a cartoon that appeared in the Brooklyn Eagle in July 1914. 'If Austria attacks Serbia, Russia will attack Austria, Germany will attack Russia, and France and Britain will attack Germany.'

Find out what the word *escalation* means. Explain why this cartoon shows the escalation of tension in Europe in 1914.

The war starts

Why did Britain join the war?

For years before the war started in 1914, Germany knew it risked having to fight a two-front war. Germany was sandwiched between France in the west and Russia in the east. These two countries were allies and were also enemies of Germany.

Germany did have a plan to deal with the two-front problem. It was called the Schlieffen Plan, named after the German chief of staff, General von Schlieffen, who created it.

The plan was to attack France hard and fast, capture Paris, surround the French armies and knock France out of the war – all within six weeks. Germany would then be free to use all of its troops to fight Russia.

The plan depended on certain things. The bulk of the German army would surprise the French by attacking through Belgium. Belgium was **neutral** and the French had no defences against an attack from Belgium.

The Germans also assumed that Belgium would allow the German troops to march through the country without objecting.

GLOSSARY
Neutral not taking sides

Activity 1

Examining visual sources

This is a cartoon called 'Bravo Belgium' that was published in the British magazine *Punch* on 4 August 1914.

▶ Which country does the man with the club represent? How do you know this? (Hint: what is in the man's pocket?)
▶ Which country does the boy represent? What is the attitude of the boy towards the man? (Hint: look at his pose in the cartoon.)
▶ What do you understand by 'no thoroughfare' on the gate behind the boy?
▶ What was the aim of the cartoonist of this piece?
▶ Draw your own sketch based on the 'Bravo Belgium' cartoon.
▶ Based on your work analysing the cartoon and your historical knowledge, prepare a report of no more than 150 words explaining why this 1914 cartoonist supported Belgium and was against Germany.

Schlieffen Plan

After France's fast defeat, the next thing the Schlieffen Plan depended on was that Russia would take a long time – about six weeks – to get its armies ready for war. The final thing it relied on was that Britain would not join the war.

Almost inevitably the plan went wrong. Russia attacked Germany more quickly than expected, so German troops had to be diverted to fight Russia instead of France. The second thing to upset the plan was that Belgium fought back and slowed down the German advance. Finally, Britain joined the war.

Seventy-five years before, in 1839, Britain and other European countries signed the Treaty of London. The treaty stated that Belgium was a neutral country and that no other European country would attack it. If one country did attack Belgium then the other countries would defend Belgium.

Of course, that was 75 years earlier and by 1914 the German Kaiser did not believe any country would bother about Belgium. He called the Treaty of London a 'scrap of paper'. He did not believe that Britain would fight. He was wrong!

Whether or not Britain really wanted to support the Treaty of London does not matter. The reality was that Britain wanted an excuse to fight Germany! The only problem was that Britain did not have a large army. All that was available was the British Expeditionary Force and the Territorial Army. They would have to face the might of the German army until a new army of volunteers could be created.

When war broke out in the summer of 1914, people in the nations of Europe were mostly happy and in Scotland young men rushed to 'join up'.

Why did the Scots join up?

The Scots had a reputation as a '**martial** race'. They were seen as natural warriors. Scots had taken part in the wars fought by Britain during the nineteenth century. The Scots stood out from other British troops because of their tartan kilts. When war broke out, posters like the one on the right tried to encourage young Scots to join the army. One way they did that was by appealing to Scottish military pride and Scottish identity.

> **GLOSSARY**
> **Martial** warlike

At the very bottom of the picture there are some words: 'A wee scrap o' paper is Britain's bond'. A bond means a promise. What do you think the 'wee scrap o' paper' refers to? Why is that included in a recruitment poster?

YOUR KING & COUNTRY NEED YOU

A WEE "SCRAP O' PAPER" IS BRITAIN'S BOND.

TO MAINTAIN THE HONOUR AND GLORY OF THE BRITISH EMPIRE

A First World War recruitment poster

Young men were encouraged to join the army. More Scots volunteered in proportion to the size of the population than in any other area of the UK. They joined up for many reasons. For some, it was peer pressure:

My real reason for joining up was a simple one. I would have been ashamed not to do so and my parents would have been ashamed of me if I had not done so.

For others, it was a desire for adventure or to earn more money and to escape conditions at home:

I was only a shop assistant at the time. I think it was more that I wanted to escape the humdrum life behind a grocer's counter and see a bit of the country.

Many believed that if they did not join up quickly, they would miss the adventure as the war would be 'over by Christmas', according to a saying of the time.

Patriotism also played a part in persuading men to fight 'for king and country'. Tales of German atrocities in Belgium convinced many that this was a war for civilisation.

In Scotland, local loyalties were also important. Regiments recruited from particular areas. The Black Watch recruited heavily from Perth and Dundee while the Cameronians concentrated in Glasgow and Lanarkshire. In Glasgow, the 'Tramway **Battalion**' was established as many of the men belonged to the transport department.

The government also encouraged recruitment. Over 54 million posters were printed, along with 8 million personal letters; over 12,000 meetings were held and 20,000 speeches were delivered by military personnel. Newspapers also encouraged men to join up and women would hand out white feathers to young men not in uniform. Criminals were also given the option to join up rather than serve a prison sentence.

The Boy's Own Paper

GLOSSARY

Patriotism love of one's country

Battalion part of an army

Martyr a person who suffers or dies for what they believe

A source of inspiration was the *Boy's Own Paper*, which was read by almost every boy in the land. Out went the jungle adventure, the narrow escapes from treacherous beasts … In came the young heroes, the barbarous Germans, the noble **martyred** French, wicked Zeppelin crews and spies. They featured in dozens of exciting stories to be rescued or outwitted by a schoolboy hero.

Off to war!

When the British Expeditionary Force (BEF) of about 120,000 soldiers left for France in August 1914, about 20,000 of them were Scots.

Most people thought the war would be 'over by Christmas'. By contrast, General Kitchener, the man in charge of the British army, believed that the war would last at least three years because of the development of ever more powerful weapons and the sheer size of the armies involved. There were some voices who spoke out against the war. In Glasgow, on 9 August 1914, there was a large anti-war demonstration attended by 5000 people.

Bertrand Russell, an anti-war campaigner, wrote the following in a letter to *The Nation* on 15 August 1914:

A month ago Europe was a peaceful group of nations: if an Englishman killed a German, he was hanged. Now, if an Englishman kills a German he is a patriot.

Such views were not popular with the majority of British people, especially as Britain had suffered 20,000 casualties in the first two weeks of the war. Nonetheless, branches of the Independent Labour Party, which opposed the war, were to be found in Dundee, Leith and Glasgow.

However, most people supported the war and by the end of August, in the Glasgow recruitment office in Gallowgate, 20,000 men had **'taken the king's shilling'**. By the end of 1915, nearly 2.5 million men had volunteered to join the British army. Thirteen per cent were Scots. One young Scottish soldier said:

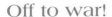

GLOSSARY

'Take the king's shilling' to join the armed forces

I enlisted on 9 September 1914 in Cambuslang. I really did not go with the intention of joining up. I just went to see the fun, because whenever a lad went to join up, the crowd would give him a hearty cheer. So after standing around for a while I must have got carried away. So in went another recruit – me! I was duly sworn in and became a soldier of the king in the Queen's Own Cameron Highlanders.

The government encouraged young men to join up together. In England these groups of friends were called 'pals' battalions' but in Scotland there were no official 'pals'. Nevertheless such groups did exist. In Glasgow, the 15th Highland Light Infantry (HLI) was made up of men from the Glasgow tramworks. Members of the Boys' Brigade formed the 16th HLI and the Chamber of Commerce provided recruits for the 17th HLI.

This was repeated across the country. In Edinburgh, men joined the 11th, 12th and 13th Royal Scots. The 15th Battalion Royal Scots was called Cranston's Battalion and the 16th Royal Scots was the McCrae's Battalion. Both were named after the commanding officers who recruited the men.

Although it seemed a good idea at the time to keep up the spirits of young men by keeping them together in friendship groups, the result of this was often that the young men who joined up together were wounded or died together. In the big battles that followed during the war, whole communities and villages were devastated by losing most of their young men.

Meanwhile, the army needed even more men and the government launched another poster campaign.

The small BEF began to cross to France on 10 August to take up its positions. This force was highly trained in rapid rifle fire and helped to slow down the German advance through Belgium.

Belgium also fought back and resisted the German advance. By slowing down the German attack and making German armies change route, they caused the carefully arranged Schlieffen Plan to go wrong!

This poster was produced as the BEF were holding up the German advance at Mons. How would you feel if you saw that poster on your way to a football match or some other leisure activity?

'Will they never come?' A First World War recruitment poster

What was the Western Front and how was it created?

The Western Front was the area in northern France and southern Belgium where millions of men fought and died over the four years of war. The Eastern Front was the scene of fighting between Russia and Germany along with Austria–Hungary. Most Scots fought on the Western Front. However, the war was never meant to be bogged down in one area. The success of the Schlieffen Plan depended on speed and it depended on France being defeated quickly. What went wrong?

As the Germans fought through Belgium, the carefully laid plans were changed to cope with the arrival of the BEF and Belgian resistance. By the time the Germans arrived in northern France they were already out of formation and behind time. When the German forces reached the River Marne, the Schlieffen Plan was in tatters.

At the Marne, British and French armies stopped the German advance. The battle involved huge numbers of men on both sides. It ended in **stalemate**, with neither side being able to land the knockout blow. However, the Germans were forced to pull back.

Both sides then tried to **outflank** their opponents without success, in what became known as 'the race to the sea'. In order to survive the hail of bullets from the enemy, men on both sides began to dig holes for protection. These holes became trenches and soon joined together to form a continuous line from the Belgian North Sea coast to the frontier of neutral Switzerland. The war on the Western Front would be fought on the same ground over and over. Stalemate was the result. After just four months of war, France alone had suffered 800,000 casualties and the BEF had practically ceased to exist. The war was not going to be over by Christmas!

GLOSSARY
Stalemate deadlock
Outflank to go round the side of the enemy

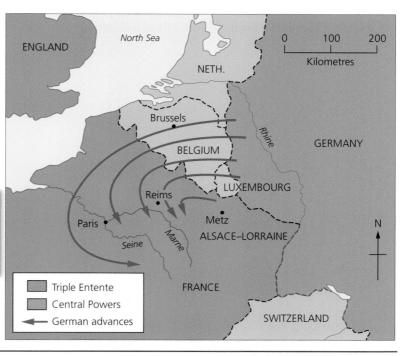

This map shows the idea behind the Schlieffen Plan. Why did so much of the success or failure of the plan depend on Belgium?

Activity 2

Question expert

This is an individual and group activity.

Your teacher will give you three sticky notes: one red, one orange and one green. You should make up three questions on the events that led to the First World War. Green should be easy (worth 1 point), orange should be more difficult (2 points) and red the most difficult (3 points). Questions should be put on the front and answers on the back of the sticky note.

Put your initials in the bottom corner of each sticky note so everyone knows who made up the question. When you are finished, put your sticky note up on the board.

Your teacher will divide you into teams. Each member of the team should take it in turns to answer questions. Everyone should try to answer at least one question. No one should answer their own questions. Each team must try to answer at least one red, one orange and one green question.

Each correct answer scores the appropriate number of points. Incorrect answers award the appropriate points to the person who made up the question.

The team with the most points wins.

Activity 3

How far can you go?

The following questions go up in level of difficulty. How many will you try to do?

1 Whose assassination helped to cause the First World War?
2 What was Austria–Hungary's reaction to the assassination?
3 Who was Austria–Hungary's ally?
4 Describe the reaction of people in Britain to the outbreak of war in 1914.
5 Explain how the assassination at Sarajevo helped to cause the First World War.
6 Explain the reasons for the failure of the Schlieffen Plan.

Activity 4

Just a minute

This is a group activity and should be done in small groups or pairs.

Your group must research topics relating to the outbreak of war and then nominate one person in your group to talk about them. Suggested topics are listed below. You can add your own topics if you wish.

- ▶ The effect of the alliance system.
- ▶ The Schlieffen Plan.
- ▶ The Treaty of London.

Planning is vital, and everyone in your group must participate. It would be helpful to assign tasks such as a researcher to get information or ideas, a timekeeper to watch how your time is being used, a facilitator to keep things running smoothly in your group (tact and diplomacy needed here!) and a recorder to note ideas before you all forget.

You must talk for a whole minute, without hesitation or repeating yourself.

If you get to the end of the minute without breaking the rules, you will get points.

Other teams can challenge you if they think you have broken the rules. If their challenge is judged to be correct, they will get a point and then can take over the remaining time. If their challenge is not correct, you will get a point and get to carry on speaking.

The team with the most points wins.

Question practice

National 4

Source A is about recruitment in Scotland.

SOURCE A

By late 1915, enthusiasm for volunteering to fight had gone. Those who had wanted to volunteer had already done so. But the scale of the task of winning the war put people off. The huge casualties in the army meant that conscription had to be introduced in early 1916.

Explain in your own words what the source tells us about Scottish recruitment. You should use Source A.

Success criteria

Include at least one piece of information about recruitment.

National 5

1 Explain the reasons why so many Scots volunteered to fight at the beginning of the First World War. (6 marks)

This is an 'explain' question. This means you must give five reasons or three developed points on why something did or did not happen. It is not enough just to write down facts, no matter how correct they are. You must make clear exactly how these facts did or did not allow something to happen. In terms of this question, your writing must use facts to show why so many Scots volunteered for the armed forces.

Here are some hints to get you started:

▶ Explain how families and communities encouraged young Scots to volunteer.
▶ Explain how patriotism and enthusiasm for king and empire encouraged young Scots to volunteer.
▶ Explain how peer pressure encouraged young Scots to volunteer.
▶ Explain how the setting up of informal 'pals' battalions' encouraged young Scots to volunteer.
▶ Explain how sports and leisure activities were used to help young Scots volunteer.

Success criteria

▶ You will need to write an introduction sentence that answers the question. For example, 'There are many reasons why so many Scots volunteered to fight at the start of the First World War.'
▶ You must give six reasons or three developed points explaining why Scots volunteered.
▶ It is not enough just to write down facts, no matter how correct they are. You must explain clearly how each fact caused young Scots to volunteer.

Source A is an account by C.N. Barclay, a Scot who enlisted for the London and Scottish Rifles, from *Scottish Voices From The Great War* by Derek Young (2005).

SOURCE A

With three or four friends I decided to join the London Scottish. My reason for doing this was that at my age and in my circumstances I would have been ashamed not to do so. My parents would have been ashamed of me if I had not done so. Other reasons were that several of my friends were joining the same regiment. Also I had already decided that I did not want to be a civil engineer. It seemed a dull sort of job.

2 How fully does Source A show the reasons why so many Scots volunteered to join the British army? Use Source A and recall to reach a judgement. (6 marks)

This is a 'how fully' question. In this type of question you need to select the points from the source which are relevant to the question – usually there will be three points in the source. Then, to get full marks, you need to bring in points from recall that are also relevant to the question.

Success criteria

▶ You will need to write an introduction sentence that gives a judgement on the question. For example, 'Source A does not fully explain why so many Scots volunteered to join the British army.'
▶ A maximum of 2 marks may be given on answers in which no judgement has been made.
▶ Up to 3 marks can be gained for explaining pieces of information from the source.

▶ Up to 4 marks can be gained for explaining pieces of information from your own knowledge which are relevant to the question asked.

▶ Pieces of information from your own knowledge can act either as further explanation of pieces of information from the source or as new points.

3 To what extent was peer pressure the main reason why Scots volunteered to fight in the First World War? (9 marks)

Planning your answer:

▶ In small groups or pairs, create a spidergram containing information on why Scots volunteered to fight in the First World War. For example, factors could include peer pressure, patriotism and recruitment campaigns.

▶ Find at least two facts per paragraph.

▶ Plan an overall response to the question.

▶ Show your plan to your teacher before starting your first draft.

▶ Read through your work carefully and mark any mistakes you spot with a green pen, then correct your work before handing it in to your teacher.

▶ Rewrite the final draft of your answer.

Success criteria

▶ One mark is available for an introduction, which should contain background and factors that you are going to write about.

▶ One mark is available for balance in your answer. This means you will have to mention at least two factors why Scots volunteered to fight during the First World War. That means at least two paragraphs of writing.

▶ This sort of question has a factor in it: in this case, it is peer pressure. You should discuss this factor first in your answer.

▶ Five marks are available for the relevant and detailed knowledge points that you are going to explain in your answer.

▶ Two marks are available for your conclusion. One mark is given for a judgement and one mark is given for a supporting reason for your conclusion.

5 What was it like for Scots fighting on the Western Front?

What is this chapter about?

As the First World War continued, trench systems became more complex. These trenches were also homes for millions of men until the end of the war. The generals tried many ways to attack trenches to defeat their enemy.

Scots played a major role during the war and the weapons they used also changed as the war progressed. Technology was increasingly used to help achieve a breakthrough on the Western Front.

By the end of this chapter you should be able to:

▶ Describe what it was like to be a Scottish soldier fighting on the Western Front.
▶ Explain how the tactics and weapons changed during the war.

How were the trenches built?

The most important feature of fighting on the Western Front was the system of trenches which ran from the North Sea coast of Belgium to the Swiss frontier. The previous chapter explained why the Western Front was created.

When the war broke out there were no trenches and no Western Front. When the Germans retreated from the River Marne, they needed to defend the territory they had already occupied so they stopped and built defensive positions in the best areas. These areas were the higher ridges overlooking the surrounding countryside. The Germans used coal miners, who were used to digging passageways, to dig their trenches. These trenches included deep dug-outs, where the men could rest and unwind. They were often reinforced with concrete.

The British and French had to build their trenches on the lower ground. This land was liable to flood. Their generals believed that the men should always be trying to go forward to push the Germans back out of France and Belgium and so British and French trenches were not nearly so well built or fortified compared to the German trenches.

During the four years that the war lasted on the Western Front, the front lines of the two sides moved only about 30 km one way or the other. Not until 1918 did the stalemate on the Western Front start to break.

As the war continued, the networks of trenches became ever more sophisticated with reserve trenches, communication trenches, their own railway system, hospitals, kitchens and defensive strong points.

Trenches were designed to give the men in them as much protection as possible. The trench was deep enough for a soldier to walk along it and not be seen by the enemy. The soil that had been dug out to form the trench was piled up in front to offer more protection. There was a firing step which allowed the men to defend their position. Wherever possible, trenches were dug in a zigzag pattern to reduce the impact from shell blasts and also prevent the enemy from invading and firing guns straight along a trench.

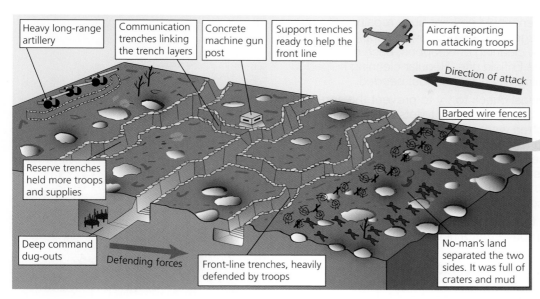

Heavy long-range artillery

Communication trenches linking the trench layers

Concrete machine gun post

Support trenches ready to help the front line

Aircraft reporting on attacking troops

Direction of attack

Barbed wire fences

Reserve trenches held more troops and supplies

Deep command dug-outs

Defending forces

Front-line trenches, heavily defended by troops

No-man's land separated the two sides. It was full of craters and mud

Using this diagram and the information in this chapter, explain why it would be difficult to break through the defensive systems of the enemy.

Trench warfare: attacking forces attempt to break through enemy trenches

A major problem facing the British forces was that of drainage. German trenches were mostly built on the high ground overlooking the British. The constant shelling of the lower area destroyed the natural drainage systems. The heavy rains of northern France led to muddy, often flooded trenches. To counteract this, **duck-boards** were placed at the bottom of the trenches to allow the men to move more freely by avoiding the mud. However, the reality was that men often stood knee deep in water for many hours.

> ### GLOSSARY
> **Duck-boards** wooden planks placed along the base of a trench
> **Censored** parts removed or cut out

What was daily life like in the trenches?

The daily life of the Scots on the Western Front was usually one of routine. The men read books, wrote letters home or played cards. All letters were **censored** so that the men did not accidentally give away information which might be useful to the enemy. At daybreak, the order to 'stand to' was given as this was when the enemy was less likely to launch an attack.

Robert MacFie, a soldier with the Liverpool Scottish, remembered his time in the trenches:

I do not think anyone can understand the wearisome monotony of fighting unless he has spent a night in the trenches. It is deadly dull, and the dullness, more than the discomfort, is what strikes me.

With the order to 'stand down' the men could relax and start to 'make a brew' (have a cup of tea) since the threat of a night attack had passed. The soldiers often complained that what they ate was boring. Bread was plentiful, as were jam and 'bully beef'. In emergencies, the men could use up their dry rations of hard biscuits but these had to be soaked in water to make them edible. Water was another problem. It had to be brought up to the front line, often in old petrol cans and the taste of the petrol remained. Often snow and ice were melted in winter to provide fresh water but occasionally the remains of a dead soldier were found in the snow.

After breakfast, the men would be kept busy repairing the trenches, filling sandbags, drilling and moving supplies. An important task was the cleaning of weapons, each man having been issued with a Lee Enfield rifle. Regular cleaning helped to prevent the rifle jamming when it was most needed.

There was a daily medical check to try to prevent the spread of disease. Trenches did not have any toilets and lack of water meant that the men often went unwashed. In such conditions, disease would spread rapidly. Despite all efforts, most men were infested with lice. This was a particular nuisance for Scots wearing kilts as the lice would live in the pleated folds at the back of the kilt. Sometimes men were sent to delousing stations but the lice soon returned.

Given the long hours that the men had to stand in waterlogged trenches, it was no surprise that a new condition appeared – **trench foot**.

In the winter of 1914–15, over 20,000 men in the British army were treated for trench foot. To reduce the problem, soldiers were ordered to keep their feet dry, to change their socks twice a day and to use whale oil to protect their feet. Andrew Gilmore, a member of the 4th Battalion Argyll and Sutherland Highlanders, wrote that about 300 members of his unit were in hospital with either trench foot or pleurisy as a result of standing knee-deep in water for four days in December 1916.

Sergeant Harry Roberts, of the Royal Army Medical Corps, wrote about trench foot in 1917:

The symptoms of trench foot and frostbite are the same. Your feet swell up to two or three times their normal size and go completely dead. You could stick a bayonet into them and not feel a thing. If you are fortunate enough not to lose your feet and the swelling begins to go down, it is then that the intolerable, indescribable agony begins. I have heard men cry and even scream with pain and many had to have their feet and legs amputated.

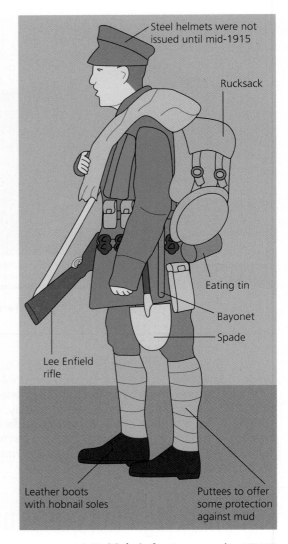

Steel helmets were not issued until mid-1915

Rucksack

Eating tin

Bayonet

Spade

Lee Enfield rifle

Leather boots with hobnail soles

Puttees to offer some protection against mud

A British infantryman in 1915

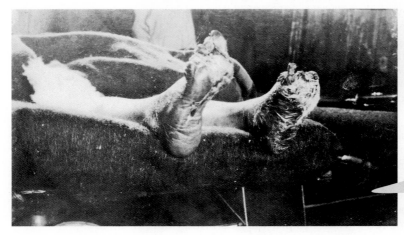

This picture shows the effects of trench foot

GLOSSARY

Trench foot an infection of the foot caused by standing in water for long periods of time

Why were military planners on both sides so concerned about the effects of trench foot on their war plans?

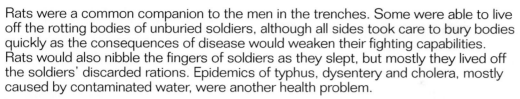

Rats were a common companion to the men in the trenches. Some were able to live off the rotting bodies of unburied soldiers, although all sides took care to bury bodies quickly as the consequences of disease would weaken their fighting capabilities. Rats would also nibble the fingers of soldiers as they slept, but mostly they lived off the soldiers' discarded rations. Epidemics of typhus, dysentery and cholera, mostly caused by contaminated water, were another health problem.

Medical care on the front line was basic. When wounded soldiers were taken back to hospitals, the treatment was better but there were no antibiotics at this time and X-rays and blood transfusions were rare. Wounded men would often die of infections.

In mid-afternoon, even in a quiet sector of the front, the Germans would bombard the British trenches for about two hours. The soldiers lived with the constant fear of death. Snipers were a real threat. The strain of living with the constant noise, gunfire and shellfire ringing in men's ears and the horrors they witnessed as pals were killed or maimed terribly was too much for some. This led many to suffer from **shell shock**. Sufferers would often react violently to any sudden noise, for example, if someone dropped a metal object onto a hard surface. During the Great War, this condition was not accepted as a real illness. Many men were dealt with harshly as it was thought they were cowards, trying to escape from the army.

> ## GLOSSARY
> **Shell shock** what is now called post-traumatic stress disorder
> **Big push** a major attack on the enemy
> **Artillery** heavy guns designed to destroy enemy positions
> **Barrage** long periods of gunfire

Evening gave the chance to sleep, but sentries had to be constantly on the alert for enemy raiding parties. Any sentry found asleep would face a court martial and if found guilty was liable to be shot. Some men had to crawl into the area between the front lines, called no-man's land, to try to capture a prisoner or to carry out repairs. At dawn, the routine was repeated.

However, it is not true that soldiers, once they arrived in the front line, stayed there for the whole war. For most of the time, any soldier in the front line could expect to be moved back to a reserve trench and then to a relaxation area within the space of two weeks. Soldiers also got leave to go home for short periods. Of course, the problem was that all soldiers eventually had to return to the horrors of the front line.

How were battles fought?

The main tactic was to try to concentrate as many men as possible in a chosen part of the front line and launch an overwhelming attack on the enemy. It was believed that a **big push** would weaken the enemy so much that they would be forced into retreat.

The planning of major battles usually followed the same pattern. After scouting out the enemy positions, often using aircraft, a good place to attack was chosen. Next the men had to be trained and prepared for battle and slowly moved to the front lines. A few days prior to the battle, the **artillery** would attempt to destroy enemy trenches. This was called an artillery **barrage**.

Before the attack started, men would crawl into no-man's land to cut a way through the barbed wire.

THE FIRST, SECOND AND THIRD ARMIES

will take steps to **DECEIVE** the enemy
as to the real front of attack,
to **WEAR HIM OUT** and
REDUCE HIS FIGHTING EFFICIENCY!

THIS WILL BE ACHIEVED BY MEANS OF:

1. Preliminary preparations such as advancing our trenches.

2. Wire cutting at intervals along the entire front to force the enemy to man his trenches and cause fatigue.

3. Gas discharges at selected points.

4. Artillery bombardments on important communications.

5. Bombardment of rest billets at night.

6. Smoke discharges and shrapnel fire to inflict losses on the enemy.

7. Night raids to assess the strength of the enemy.

The battle orders of General Haig issued in May 1916, just before the Battle of the Somme

At **zero hour**, officers would blow whistles and the men had to be ready to scramble up ladders out of their trenches and advance across no-man's land against heavy enemy fire. It was likely that the attacking men would be cut down by machine guns or killed by enemy artillery soon after leaving their trenches. The barbed wire defences which both sides used to protect their trenches meant many soldiers became entangled and were then easy targets. Others slid or crawled into water-filled shell holes where they often drowned or died of their wounds, as there was little chance of being rescued.

As the war continued, it became obvious that such tactics were not breaking through the enemy defences. Nonetheless, this type of warfare continued until late into the war and, although losses were huge, the tactics of **attrition** were eventually successful. Attrition meant wearing the enemy down, soldier by soldier, bullet by bullet, until one side had nothing left. By 1918, Germany was exhausted. The final straw for Germany was when the USA joined the war. The Americans brought fresh new troops and supplies when Germany had nothing left to give.

General Douglas Haig was the British army's leader of the war effort from 1915 until its conclusion. He was promoted to the rank of Field Marshal, the highest rank in the British army, in 1917.

GLOSSARY

Zero hour the exact time an attack is launched

Attrition wearing down the enemy

Troops going over the top, *a 1914 painting*

Draw a sketch diagram of this scene. On your drawing, add numbered arrows pointing to six important features of an attack.

Haig was born in Edinburgh in 1861. At the beginning of the war he thought that the **cavalry** would play an important part in the war effort. However, he underestimated the impact of modern weapons such as machine guns and tanks. His handling of the Battle of the Somme in 1916 and the Battle of Passchendaele in 1917 met with heavy criticism by military historians. The British army suffered huge losses in these battles due in part to Haig's policy of attrition.

However, Haig also changed his tactics. In 1916 both sides began to use what became known as a creeping barrage.

First used at the Battle of the Somme, a creeping barrage involved artillery fire moving forward in stages, just ahead of the advancing infantry. By the autumn, the Allied forces developed a system where the barrage moved forward at 50 metres per minute. To work, the strategy required precise timing by both the heavy artillery and the infantry. Failure to do this would result in the artillery killing their own soldiers. By the end of the war Haig was using combinations of tanks, soldiers, aircraft and radio communications to launch successful attacks against the enemy.

GLOSSARY
Cavalry soldiers on horseback

Haig remains a controversial figure to this day. His supporters point to the reality of trench warfare, which was a long, drawn-out affair and involved heavy losses. New technology was slow to develop and many of the troops were inexperienced, often no more than boys. Could he have done anything else at the Somme than ask the Kitchener volunteers to march forward bravely? His opponents argue that his tactics wasted hundreds of thousands of lives.

The contribution of the Scots on the Western Front

Scottish regiments played a significant role in many of the battles on the Western Front. Three of the main battles, at Loos in 1915, the Somme in 1916 and Arras in 1917, will be analysed to show the way in which the war changed.

The table below shows the number of Scots who served in the various branches of the armed forces during the war.

Branch of armed services	Number of Scots who served
Regular Army and Territorial Army	584,098
Royal Navy and allied services	71,707
RFC/RAF	32,611
Total	**688,416**

From *The Great War and the British People*, 2nd edition, JM Winter, Palgrave, 2003.

The Battle of Loos, 1915

The Battle of Loos in 1915 became famous for its involvement of large numbers of Scots.

Scottish battalions made up half the number involved in this battle. With 30,000 troops, this was the greatest number ever to fight together in the British army. Gas was also used by the British for the first time but with little success. On the first day, the troops of the 15th Scottish Division captured the village of Loos, but they had to return to their original positions after only four days. This was due to exhaustion, the reserve troops being too far back to help and the Germans holding the high ground. The battle was indecisive and brought the end of the war no closer.

Scottish losses among regiments like the Cameronians, Black Watch and the Gordon Highlanders were so high that nearly every part of the country was affected. Seven Scottish battalions lost their commanding officers. Eight out of the twelve battalions which lost over 500 men were Scottish. On the Memorial to the Missing at Loos, of the 20,598 names listed, one in three is Scottish. Despite the failure of the attack, Scots took pride in their fighting during the battle and morale was kept high.

Five Scots were awarded the Victoria Cross for valour during the battle. The courage of Piper Daniel Laidlaw was shown in the **citation** for his award. It read as follows:

GLOSSARY

Citation special statement commending bravery

For most conspicuous bravery during an assault on German trenches near Loos and Hill 70 on 25 September 1915.
During the worst of the bombardment, Piper Laidlaw, seeing his company was badly shaken by the effects of gas, with absolute coolness and disregard of danger, mounted the parapet, marched up and down and played the company out of the trench. The effect of his splendid example was immediate and the company dashed out to the assault. Piper Laidlaw continued playing his pipes until he was wounded.

There was a high price to pay for such acts of gallantry. This description is from *The Regimental History of the Black Watch*:

The 4th Black Watch had lost very heavily; all its officers had been killed or wounded with three exceptions. The losses were so severe that it was now amalgamated temporarily with the 2nd Battalion Black Watch.

To many at home, this huge loss of life came as a shock.

The Battle of the Somme, 1916

The following year, the Scots again played a major role, in the Battle of the Somme. Part of the battle's aim was to help the French allies who had been attacked at the fortress town of Verdun from February 1916. Three Scottish Divisions, the 9th and 15th Scottish and the 51st (Highland) Division, attacked during the early part of the offensive. In total, 51 Scottish infantry battalions were involved between July and November 1916. Over 600,000 casualties were suffered by the British army, 60,000 on the first day, of which 20,000 were killed.

Trevor Royle in *The Flowers of the Forest* tells of the Scottish attitude to fighting:

The 16th Highland Light Infantry – the 'Boys' Brigade' battalion (which had been recruited from the Glasgow area) – attacked at Beaumont Hamel. Three platoons from 'D' Company attacked the 'Frankfurt' trench. However, they were left behind with men from the 11th Borderers when the rest of the army withdrew. This left around 100 men, half of them injured, with four Lewis machine-guns. They held out against repeated German attacks for a week after the original attack. They had no food or water for several days. When they were eventually captured on 25 November, only 15 were able to fight and 30 were wounded.

How the battle might have been reported in a modern-day tabloid newspaper

General Haig hoped to capture the German lines by using overwhelming force against them. The British artillery attack, which was intended to destroy the enemy front line trenches and lower the defenders' morale, lasted a week. When the British attacked, they would be supported by a creeping barrage. The artillery would fire just ahead of the advancing soldiers. This would stop the Germans from reinforcing their front line. Although this tactic was successful against clearly defined and local targets, overall it failed because of a lack of co-ordination among all those involved.

Here are some results of the Battle of the Somme:

◗ 600,000 Allied casualties
◗ pressure taken off the French at Verdun
◗ not much land gained
◗ valuable lessons learned in artillery and tactics, including the use of tanks
◗ the 51st Highland Division attacked in November, capturing Beaumont Hamel
◗ the spirit of the German army was weakened.

Activity 1

Class debate

Organise a class debate on the British attack on the Somme. The theme of the debate is 'The Scots made an important contribution to the fighting on the Western Front'.

Two students must put forward the case in favour of this theme and two must speak against it.

At the end of the debate, and after a question and answer session, the class will vote. The winner is the side with the greater number of votes.

Arras, 1917

By 1917, the British army had become a strong fighting force. In April 1917, they moved into the area around the French town of Arras. The battle which followed probably contained more Scots fighting in one place than at any point during the war. Ten Scottish divisions fought at Arras with nearly one-third of the 159,000 casualties being Scots.

Because of new tactics and skilled artillery fire, the attack was much more successful than at Loos. The artillery did its job well. Shells cut the wire and gas shells killed German transport horses, which made moving guns impossible. The attack was well planned with many troops moved up to the assault line in secret. Artillery was accurate and pinned down the German defenders. Troops used a new method of attack. Instead of a wave of soldiers attacking all at once, one part would advance. It would then consolidate the ground it had captured. Another part of the army would then continue the attack and this was repeated over and over.

Such assaults taught the British lessons. By 1918, the British had developed the 'all arms battle plan'. Infantry, artillery, tanks and aircraft were used together in attack. This strategy helped to win the war.

Activity 2

What was trench warfare like?

You should work in pairs or small groups. Research and deliver a presentation about trench warfare to your classmates. The presentation can be a PowerPoint if you wish. It should not last more than five minutes.

You will need to listen to everyone's presentation and give it a red, amber or green rating depending on whether you think the presentation has met the following success criteria:

▶ Did the presentation include a labelled diagram of a trench system?
▶ Did the presentation explore the problems of attacking a trench system?
▶ Did the presentation include key information about trenches, trench warfare, conditions and experiences?

After you have seen all the presentations, hold a class discussion on key information you have learned about trench warfare.

Technology of war

It was not just the way in which the war was fought that changed between 1914 and 1918. New weapons were also introduced by both sides in an effort to break the stalemate on the Western Front.

The First World War was the first war between industrialised countries. Vast quantities of munitions could be produced quickly. Aerial observation using planes and balloons changed the way intelligence was gathered about the enemy. Field telephones meant it was quicker and easier to send and receive signals from headquarters. The railways made it easier to keep large numbers of men supplied and equipped all year round.

In addition to their field rifles, soldiers were issued with hand grenades, such as the Mills bomb, which were used in close-combat fighting. Mortars were also used to shell the enemy defences, as these had a range of 1000 metres. Both sides used machine guns, which were an excellent defensive weapon. A Vickers machine gun could fire 500 bullets a minute. This resulted in heavy losses to an attacking force.

Artillery

Artillery was used before and during an attack. As the war progressed, its range and accuracy improved greatly. This allowed the introduction of the 'creeping barrage' in 1916. The idea was that the artillery would fire just ahead of the attacking infantry to keep the enemy soldiers pinned down until the attacking force was on them. However, if the range was incorrect, this would lead to **blue on blue** casualties with men being wounded or killed by their own artillery. More soldiers were killed by artillery fire than by any other weapon on the Western Front.

> **GLOSSARY**
> **Blue on blue** soldiers killed or wounded accidentally by their own side

Create a spidergram of the difficulties of trench warfare illustrated in this picture.

First World War artillery at work

Gas

In a desperate attempt to break the deadlock on the Western Front, both sides used poison gas. At Ypres in Belgium in the spring of 1915, the Germans first used chlorine gas against British and Canadians. However, gas was an unpredictable weapon. A change in wind direction meant the gas could blow back on the men who had released it, as Scottish soldiers at Loos found out. This problem was solved by 1916 when gas-filled shells replaced gas cylinders.

At first, soldiers had no protection against gas. However, it was soon discovered that a moistened cloth over the mouth could provide some protection. If all else failed, the men had to urinate on handkerchiefs and hold the wet cloth to their faces as a form of protection! However, gas soon became a less effective weapon as both sides developed gas masks.

Use the internet to search for information on the various types of poison gases used and how they worked. Describe, in as much detail as you can, their effectiveness as a weapon.

Contemporary view of German troops in gas masks

Different types of gas were developed. Chlorine gas caused lung damage as the gas formed an acid when inhaled. This was usually fatal, with an often slow and very painful death. Phosgene gas also destroyed the lungs but was invisible and therefore more dangerous than the greenish-yellow smog of chlorine gas. Finally, mustard gas blistered exposed skin and caused blindness. It also resulted in both internal and external bleeding.

Private W. Hay of the Royal Scots arrived in Ypres just after the chlorine gas attack on 22 April 1915:

We knew there was something wrong. We started to march towards Ypres but we couldn't get past on the road with refugees coming down the road. There were people, civilians and soldiers, lying along the roadside in a terrible state. We heard them say it was gas. We didn't know what the hell gas was. When we got to Ypres we found a lot of Canadians lying there dead from gas the day before, poor devils, and it was quite a horrible sight for us young men. I was only twenty so it was quite traumatic and I've never forgotten nor ever will forget it.

John Singer Sargent's Gassed *shows temporarily blinded soldiers walking from the battlefield*

Tanks

With both sides dug into strong defensive networks of trenches, there was stalemate on the Western Front. Neither side could break through and the war remained static.

The idea of a tank had been imagined as early as 1902, but no one had taken it seriously. It was based on pre-war tractors with caterpillar tracks which were used on muddy fields. However, with the Western Front bogged down in its own gigantic, muddy field, tanks were once again being tested.

The first tanks were called 'land ships' and could travel no faster than walking pace. However, they could climb steep slopes and cross gaps of about 2.5 metres, the average width of a trench. Their firing range was about 30 km and the crew was made up of ten men. The first prototype was nicknamed 'Little Willie', making fun of the German Kaiser, Wilhelm. When they proved their worth, 150 were ordered and sent to France covered in tarpaulins labelled 'water tanks' to keep them secret from the Germans. The name 'tank' stuck.

It was at the Battle of Cambrai in November 1917 that tanks showed their true worth. Here the ground was firm and not too badly affected by shellfire. On 20 November 1917, 378 tanks supported by 289 aircraft attacked the German trenches. Many tanks carried huge rolls of tightly packed brushwood called **fascines** to drop into trenches to help tanks cross them. Tanks operated in small groups and when one tank dropped its fascine, others would cross and drop their fascines in the next line of trenches.

GLOSSARY

Fascines bundles of wood used to fill in trenches

At first, the attack went well with the British forces creating a hole in the German lines about 11 km wide and 6 km deep. However, the success did not last long as there were not enough soldiers to follow the tanks and break through into the gap. The tanks also began to break down. In total, 165 tanks either ran out of fuel or had mechanical problems. Gradually, the Germans pushed the British forces back.

Nonetheless, the tank had given people a glimpse of future warfare. From then on, tanks were used wherever the ground was suitable.

How would attackers and defenders feel if they were in this battlefield situation?

A First World War tank in action

Aeroplanes

In 1903, Orville and Wilbur Wright had flown in the first ever machine-powered aircraft. Only 11 years later, planes were being used in the war. At first, the role of the plane was mostly intelligence-gathering. At the Battle of the Marne in 1914, a pilot spotted a gap between the advancing German armies and the British and French quickly pushed into it, forcing the Germans to retreat.

Dogfights

The first fighter planes were only equipped with machine guns, which were fixed onto the top wing. These early fighter aircraft had two seats, with the man sitting in the rear controlling the guns. Dogfights were extremely difficult because the pilot would have to dodge other enemy aircraft while listening to the commands of the gunner as to where to fly to get the enemy into his sights.

Anton Fokker developed a machine gun which could fire through revolving propeller blades. By the autumn of 1915, Fokker was fitting his monoplanes with this so-called 'interrupter gear', thereby producing the first true fighter aircraft. It was now possible for a pilot in a single-seater aircraft to fire a machine gun successfully.

Almost all the pilots involved in flying aircraft in the First World War were under the age of 25. As the death rate was very high, by 1918 a large proportion of the pilots were aged between 18 and 21. Pilots were sent into combat after only around 30 hours of air training. Training in how to take part in dogfights had to be given by the more experienced pilots at the battle front.

In Scotland, the demand for this new weapon of war led to the expansion of Beardmore's steelworks in the east end of Glasgow into aircraft and airship production at Dalmuir and Inchinnan. The aircraft they built included the Sopwith Pup fighters, Wight seaplanes and the giant four-engined Handley Page V/1500 bombers. A steel-framed airship hangar at Inchinnan was created to build airships.

Newspaper drawing of an aerial battle

Eventually, there were different types of aircraft used for specific purposes. Fighter planes were fast, manoeuvrable and fitted with machine guns. Heavier planes were designed to carry bombs. **Reconnaissance** or scouting planes were flown over enemy lines to gather information about enemy placements. By 1918, planes had been developed which could carry heavy bombs to attack Germany's capital of Berlin.

Activity 3

Summarise this chapter

Answer one or both of these questions. The first question will help you to plan your answer to the second.

1 Give at least one reason why the weapons listed below caused so many deaths:
 ▶ artillery
 ▶ machine guns
 ▶ gas
 ▶ tanks
 ▶ aeroplanes.

2 Why was it so hard to 'break through' an opponent's trench system? (Use all the information in the chapter to help you answer this question.)

Question practice

National 4

Source A is about the experience of Scottish soldiers on the Western Front. It is by a Scot, 2nd Lieutenant Crerar.

SOURCE A

We set off for the front line and had a tiring, slow journey in full kilts, rifle, etc., up communication trenches, sometimes under quite heavy shellfire. The next four days were the most miserable I have experienced in my long life. Our trench was almost constantly under heavy shellfire as were the communication trenches which prevented rations getting to us. It was often raining.

1 Describe the effects of the fighting on Scottish soldiers on the Western Front. You should use Source A and your own knowledge.

Success criteria

Include at least two points or one developed piece of information about the effect of fighting on the Western Front on Scottish soldiers.

Source B is about conditions in the trenches for Scottish soldiers. It is by Norman Collins from the Seaforth Highlanders.

SOURCE B

When we entered the trench, it had been very battered by all the fighting. As we went, I noticed that the trenches had parts of bodies sticking out of the wall for quite a long way. I suppose the trench had been dug through where the bodies lay. Sometimes, you would see a loose head or two lying about.

Source C is about conditions in the trenches. It is by Lieutenant Sotheby from the Argyll and Sutherland Highlanders who fought with the Black Watch.

SOURCE C

The flies here are terrible. Huge numbers fly before you whenever you walk about. Dead bodies lay about unburied and the smell is awful. This part of the ground has been fought over many times and so is quite poor. It is impossible to bury people properly.

2 Compare the views in Sources B and C about conditions in the trenches. Describe in detail their similarities and/or differences. You can also briefly compare the overall attitude of the sources.

Success criteria

▶ Examine the two sources in order to show two simple points of comparison or one developed point of similarity or difference.
▶ A simple comparison: 'Source B says … and Source C says …'.
▶ A developed comparison: 'Sources B and C agree that the ground in the trenches had suffered because of all the fighting. Source B says … and Source C says …'.

National 5

Source A is about the attack of the Black Watch regiment at Loos, 1915.

SOURCE A

The Black Watch marched with determination. They got into the German line, but were unsupported. Two companies disappeared and the remainder were sorely shattered. The whole affair was absolute carnage. The second attack was just murder, sending brave men to certain death, and, my God, they met it like men, too.

Source B is about the attack of the Black Watch regiment at Loos, 1915, as reported in a German newspaper.

SOURCE B

Then the British came through with tremendous fierceness. They sent in one of their best Highland regiments to the front, the best they have anywhere. The Black Watch advanced. The gallant Scots came on and even managed to get in our trench, but even their really heroic bravery was in vain, for they were not able to turn the fate of the day.

1 Compare the views of Sources A and B about the attack of the Black Watch at Loos. (4 marks)

Success criteria

▶ You should interpret evidence from the sources.
▶ Make direct comparisons between the information in the sources.
▶ You can get up to 4 marks for making four simple comparisons between the information in the two sources.
▶ You can get up to 4 marks for making two developed comparisons between the information in the two sources.
▶ A simple comparison: 'Source A says … and Source B says …' will get 1 mark.
▶ A developed comparison: 'Sources A and B agree about the fierce way in which the Black Watch fought. Source A says … and Source B says …' will get 2 marks.

2 How important was the Scots contribution to the fighting on the Western Front? (9 marks)

Planning your answer:

▶ In small groups or pairs, create a spidergram containing information on why Scots were important to the fighting and the ways in which they were not.
▶ Group the information into two paragraphs. Paragraph one: 'Importance to fighting'. For example, Battle of Loos and Somme, leadership of Douglas Haig. Paragraph two: 'Limits to importance to fighting'. For example, small numbers, limited success of Loos and Somme.
▶ Find connections between the different pieces of information and join them together. This will give you a structure for the order in which you talk about the significance of the Scottish contribution to the fighting.
▶ Plan an overall response to the question.
▶ Show your plan to your teacher before starting your first draft.
▶ Read through your work carefully and mark any mistakes you spot with a green pen, then correct your work before handing it to your teacher.
▶ Rewrite the final draft of your answer.

Success criteria

▶ One mark is available for an introduction, which should contain background and factors that you are going to write about.
▶ One mark is available for balance in your answer. This means you will have to mention at least two factors discussing the importance of the Scottish contribution to the fighting on the Western Front. That means at least two paragraphs of writing.
▶ This sort of question does not have a factor in it. In paragraph one, you need to make sure you discuss the ways in which the contribution of the Scots to the fighting was important. In the second paragraph, you should discuss the ways in which the Scottish contribution was not important.
▶ Five marks are available for the relevant and detailed knowledge points that you are going to explain in your answer.
▶ Two marks are available for your conclusion. One mark is given for a judgement and one mark is given for a supporting reason for your conclusion.

Domestic impact of war: society and culture

6 How did the war affect people back at home?

What is this chapter about?

For the first time ever in Britain, the whole population became in involved in the effort to win the war. Both men and women worked in essential war industries and in farming. Civilians became targets for enemy action. This was called the 'home front'. The home front means how the war affected everyday life for civilians back home.

By the end of this chapter you should be able to:

▶ Describe how the war affected people at home.
▶ Explain the ways in which the government controlled the lives of British citizens during the war.
▶ Describe how the people of Scotland marked the deaths of their loved ones.

Government control: Defence of the Realm Act

On 8 August 1914, the British government passed the Defence of the **Realm** Act (DORA). This gave the government the power to direct men, women and materials to areas where they were most needed to help with the war effort.

Military laws

Under DORA, railways and docks came under military law. Special police constables were recruited to enforce the new laws. All non-military vehicles were to be put out of action if Britain was invaded. Later in the war, air-raid precautions were introduced and windows had to be 'blacked out' at night.

The government was also able to send workers to work in industries where they were required. In Scotland, many single women were sent to the munitions factory at Gretna.

Alcohol

The government was also concerned about the effect of drunkenness. It worried that drunk workers would not do a good job and so, to prevent lost production in war industries, the government took control of pubs in some areas and reduced the opening hours of all pubs. Alcohol could only be sold between 12 noon and 2.30 p.m. and 6.30 p.m. and 9.00 p.m. Pubs were also forbidden to open on Sundays. This led to much bitterness. David Lloyd George, a leading wartime politician, blamed the problems in ammunition production on the heavy drinking of workers in the west of Scotland. Tax on alcohol also increased and the new rules seemed to work. Convictions for drunkenness in Scotland fell by 70 per cent by the end of the war.

Censorship

Under DORA, censorship was introduced in 1914 to stop newspapers printing information which might be helpful to the enemy.

Land use

In Scotland, and other parts of Britain, DORA allowed local councils to take over land and to use this to grow more food.

In the Highlands of Scotland, this had an impact on the old issue of land ownership. Landowners had used much of their land for things like deer forests and grouse shooting on the moors. During war this was not useful. DORA allowed local crofters access to this land to grow food. After the war, these crofting tenants were supposed to hand the land back to the landowners, but they did not always do this.

Alien registration

As well as powers under DORA, the government also introduced the Alien Registration Act in 1914. This required all foreign citizens to register as **aliens** at their local police station. Restrictions were placed on where aliens could travel, changes of address had to be notified to the police and any suspicious activity would be investigated. Failure to register could lead to a fine or imprisonment.

Propaganda

To win the support of the British people, the government started a **propaganda** campaign to persuade them to back the war effort.

Sketches showing the Germans killing civilians were produced in newspapers. No photographs of these events were published as most of them never actually took place. However, the campaign to gain support for the war effort was successful. Anti-German feeling grew so strong that even the British Royal Family was affected. It changed its name from Saxe-Coburg Gotha to the House of Windsor. German civilians living in Britain were arrested as aliens and put in prison for the rest of the war.

There were stories of Dachshund dogs (originally bred in Germany) being beaten up in the streets. At Christmas, people refused to sing German-language carols such as *Silent Night* and people refused to attend concerts featuring the works of German composers like Bach and Beethoven.

> **GLOSSARY**
> **Propaganda** information to influence public opinion

> After seeing this poster, what would people's reaction be to supporting the war effort? What would their attitude be towards the Germans for doing this?

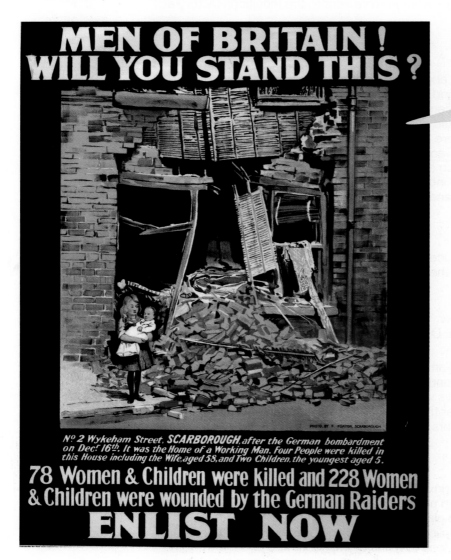

An example of Anti-German propaganda

The changing role of women

The impact of the First World War on the political role of women will be dealt with later, in Chapter 7.

It was the role of women which underwent the greatest change during the war, although this was mostly temporary. Before the war, women were thought to be unable to do the same work as men. Many men (and women) thought that a woman's place was in the home. The 1911 Scottish census showed that over half of women working did so as servants in houses or making cloth and clothing. Less than ten per cent of women worked as nurses, as professionals or in offices. The need to increase production of weapons, however, led to a dramatic change.

Year	Women employed in heavy industry in Scotland
1911	3,758
1916	18,500
1918	31,500

Employment of women in Scotland for 1911, 1916 and 1918

Industry	Number of women
Munitions	819,000
Engineering	800,000
Government work	650,000
Nursing	100,000

Number of female workers in Britain in 1917

> Look at the figures in the two tables. In what ways did the work of women change during the war?

Women filled many jobs brought into existence by wartime needs. As a result, the number of women employed increased from 3,224,600 in July 1914 to 4,814,600 in January 1918.

Women worked as conductors on trams and buses. Industries that had previously excluded women now welcomed them. There was a particular demand for women to do heavy work such as unloading coal, stoking furnaces and building ships.

The employment of women released men for the armed services but, more importantly, made a valuable contribution to the war effort. The pay and overtime were also good and many women found that they were better off during the war than before.

Women also gained much more freedom. Good wages meant women could go to the cinema or shopping in town. This war work also contributed towards some women gaining the vote in 1918.

Women working in munitions factories

During the war, making explosives and shells was among the most dangerous work women did. At Gretna, in south-west Scotland, a huge **cordite** factory was built. In fact, the town of Gretna was deliberately built up to house the workers of the factory nearby. There were 9000 women and 5000 men employed there. A typical shift would last 12 hours with 90 minutes for meal breaks. The work was dangerous, with women being told to remove hairpins and anything else that might cause a spark that could lead to an explosion. Even with these precautions, one woman was killed in an explosion in 1917, but Gretna was seen as one of the safer munitions factories.

> **GLOSSARY**
> **Cordite** explosive used in ammunition

What rules would your class make to ensure least possible risk to the workers?

Female munitions workers producing heavy artillery shells

Dilution

Another major issue facing female workers was the argument over **dilution**. Skilled men had had to serve an apprenticeship of seven years before they were fully qualified. By contrast, women were only given a few weeks' training. Those skilled men who had not gone to fight objected to women and semi-skilled men being paid the same wages as themselves.

> **GLOSSARY**
>
> **Dilution** replacing skilled workmen with semi-skilled or unskilled workers

In what ways does this poster encourage women to be part of the war effort?

The solution was to introduce a scheme known as dilution. This was set up by the Ministry of Munitions in 1915. This scheme broke down skilled jobs into separate parts. Women were trained to complete some of these parts but not all. In that way, neither the skilled man's status nor his wages were threatened.

Despite women's valuable wartime contribution, they did face many difficulties. Women were not paid the same wages as men for doing the same work. Also, the woman's employment was only temporary. The government had promised the men fighting in the war that they would have their former jobs back once the war was over. The passing of the Pre-War Practices Act meant that women would be forced to leave their jobs to give them back to the returning soldiers. As Trevor Royle wrote in *The Flowers of the Forest*:

The female wartime experience was only temporary and in the post-war years this meant a return to women's work, usually low paid and repetitive.

Rationing

Women had to 'keep the home fires burning'. Before 1914, 60 per cent of food eaten in Britain came from overseas. Germany tried to stop food coming to Britain. In 1915 and again in 1917, German submarines attacked ships bringing essential supplies.

A poster produced during the war showing the impact of rationing

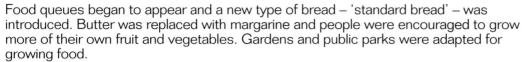

Food queues began to appear and a new type of bread – 'standard bread' – was introduced. Butter was replaced with margarine and people were encouraged to grow more of their own fruit and vegetables. Gardens and public parks were adapted for growing food.

Across Britain, 250,000 women joined the Land Army. These women replaced the male farm workers who had gone off to war. Despite all these efforts, the government had to introduce rationing in December 1917 to ensure that everyone received an equal share of food.

Foodstuffs	Percentage increase in price between 1914 and 1916
General foodstuffs	65%
Sugar	166%
Fish and eggs	100%
Flour	66%
Margarine	19%
Milk	39%
Potatoes	53%

This table shows the impact which food shortages had on the price of foodstuffs. Figures from the Board of Trade, October 1916 (as noted by Trevor Royle in *The Flowers of the Forest*)

People received ration cards and these cards named the shop where the holder could buy specific items. The shopkeeper stamped the card to show that the week's supply had been purchased. The system worked reasonably well but those who could afford to were able to buy additional goods on the thriving '**black market**'. By 1918, food shortages resulted in the introduction of two 'meat-less' days per week, Scotland's being Wednesday and Friday, when it became illegal to serve meat at any meal in any public place such as a hotel or restaurant.

GLOSSARY

Black market the illegal sale of things that should have been rationed

The direct contribution of Scottish women to the war effort

Scottish Women's Hospitals were the idea of Dr Elsie Inglis, who had been a campaigner for the vote before 1914. She suggested setting up the field hospitals near the front line. This was one way in which women who wanted to contribute to the war effort could do so in a positive way. The idea was rejected by the British government. However, the French and Serbian governments were more enthusiastic and Dr Inglis helped to raise money to set up hospitals in both France and Serbia. One French hospital treated over 10,000 servicemen. She herself saw active service with both the Serbian and Russian forces. Indeed, it was while she was returning from Russia to Scotland in November 1917 that Elsie died. She was given a full military funeral in Edinburgh.

In the short term, Elsie's work, and that of her supporters, provided much needed medical assistance to Britain's allies. In the long term, the Scottish Women's Hospitals, and other voluntary women's hospitals, showed that not only could women cope with the demands of military medicine, but that they could also work under stressful and trying conditions.

Ishobel Ross, a volunteer at one of the hospitals in Serbia, wrote a diary of her experiences. Here is her entry from 19 September 1916:

The wounded have been coming in all day, nearly all frightfully bad cases. From the window we can see the ambulances arriving at the reception tent, and the poor men carried in. All the Serbs working in the camp are so pleased to have

the hospital started at last, and indeed we are too. Three of the men, very badly wounded in the head, died tonight. We get the worse cases here and some of the wounded have been lying untended for two days.

The contribution of these women was noted by a Serbian government official commenting on the Women's Medical Unit working at Costanza (1917):

It is extraordinary how these women endure hardships; they refuse help and carry the wounded themselves. They work like navvies. No wonder Britain is a great country if the women are like that.

This contribution was also recognised at home. The following is an extract from the *Glasgow Herald*, dated 22 September 1917:

The splendid work performed by the Scottish Women's Hospitals in Serbia and Salonika during the devastating period of the war has been one of the brightest chapters. It brings into relief the nobility and innate capacity of the Scottish women who have been called upon to stay in the immediate battle area.

Staff of the Scottish Women's Hospitals on service in 1915

> Search the internet to find out more about what the Scottish Women's Hospitals provided during the war.

Mairi Chisholm was another example of a Scottish woman who made a positive contribution to the war. Aged just 18, she cycled to London and was recruited by Dr Hector Munro, who was organising a medical team to go to Belgium. For the next 18 months, Dr Munro and his team supplied medical aid to the Belgian people. In January 1915, Mairi was honoured by the King of the Belgians in recognition of her contribution. In March 1918, Mairi was the victim of a gas attack and returned to Scotland at the end of that month. Of her adventures, she wrote:

Three and a half years of being privileged to work in the danger alongside brave men. The cause was greater than ourselves.

Conscription

At first there was great enthusiasm for the war and men rushed to enlist. However, there were some people who were against the war. Later, as the reality of trench warfare became clearer and the thousands of early volunteers were killed, the government had to use **conscription** to get men into the armed forces.

Key laws

▶ National Registrations Act, July 1915. All people, men and women, to be registered for possible service.
▶ Military Service Acts, January and May 1916 and 1918:
  – the first Act conscripted all single men and childless widowers, aged 18–41
  – the second Act included married men
  – the third Act in 1918 increased the age limit to 51.

Conscription led to renewed opposition to the war by some groups and individuals.

Why did some people oppose the war?

Most people supported the war and conscription because they thought it was necessary for the war effort. However, some opposed the war for political or religious reasons. One important political reason was **socialism**. Many Scots were members of a small political party called the Independent Labour Party (ILP). Its members believed that the war had been started by **capitalists**. It was working men who fought and died – not the bosses and owners of factories. The ILP opposed the war because they believed that working men were being exploited.

Other men opposed the war for religious reasons. Many believed it was against their religion to kill; one such group was the Quakers. Such ideas, however, were not popular.

Only a few people opposed conscription. Early in 1915, a branch of the No Conscription Fellowship (NCF) was opened in Glasgow. The NCF often worked closely with the ILP as they both opposed conscription. Opponents to conscription were accused of being unpatriotic. Those who opposed the war because of their socialist ideals found little sympathy at the military tribunals set up to hear their cases.

During the war years, over 16,000 men refused to serve in the armed forces. They argued that it was against their moral or religious beliefs to fight. They were known as conscientious objectors or 'conchies' for short. The conscientious objectors thought the term conchie was offensive. Most of these men were prepared to help the war effort by doing **non-combatant** jobs such as carrying stretchers and driving ambulances.

A small minority of conscientious objectors refused to do anything that would support the war effort. They were known as 'absolutists' and they faced harsh consequences. They were sent to prison by the military tribunals that heard their cases. Some 6261 were imprisoned or forced to do hard labour. Of these, 71 died as a result of their treatment and another 31 were declared insane. One description said there were some shameful cases of sadistic treatment. A modern historian wrote the following about the treatment of some conscientious objectors during the war:

One inmate, told he would be executed, was taken through the motions of an actual execution, to the point of the gun being loaded and pointed at him. Inmates were force-fed, tied into straitjackets, beaten, kept in filthy cells, fed on bread and water and often tortured.

Compulsory military service ended in December 1920.

> **GLOSSARY**
>
> **Conscription** compulsory military service
>
> **Socialism** a political movement aiming to create an equal society
>
> **Capitalists** people who owned factories, businesses and transport and who ran these for private profit
>
> **Non-combatant** a soldier who does not take part in the fighting

A nation mourns

By 1918, nearly every family in Britain was mourning the loss of a relative. The traditional signs of mourning were the lowering of window blinds and the wearing of black clothes on Sundays.

Families found out what happened to their relatives in different ways. Officially, the army would send a telegram. Often friends of the killed soldier would send letters home. Army chaplains would also write letters to the bereaved. The officer commanding the man who had died might write a letter of **condolence**. During the major battles, local newspapers would publish lists of those killed and wounded. Frequently whole streets and villages lost most of their young men as those who had joined up together often died together.

> **GLOSSARY**
>
> **Condolence** expression of sympathy over a death

The exact number of Scots who died in the First World War will probably never be known. The official figure produced at the end of the conflict was 74,000. Others believe the number is somewhere between 100,000 and 150,000. In *The Flowers of the Forest*, the historian Trevor Royle has given some idea of the scale of casualties and deaths suffered by some of the Scots Regiments during the war.

Regiment	Casualty figures
The Royal Scots	11,213
The Black Watch	10,000
The Highland Light Infantry	10,000
The Gordons	9,000

13,568 men volunteered from Scotland's four universities, with 2026 killed on active service – almost 15 per cent.

Glasgow lost 18,888 young men while in Dundee 4213 men were killed out of a city population of 180,000. Each individual's death was a loss to a family, a community and the nation. On the next page is an example of the type of letter which was sent to inform loved ones of the death of their relatives on active service.

Army Form B. 104—82

Infantry Record Office,

Aberdeen

May 9ᵗʰ 1917

Madam

It is my painful duty to inform you that a report has been received from the War Office notifying the death of:—

(No.) *1245920* (Rank) *Private*

(Name) *Bertie Albert Gray*

(Regiment) *Gordon Highlanders*

which occurred *at place not stated*

on the *16ᵗʰ April 1917*

The report is to the effect that he *was*

Killed in action

By His Majesty's command I am to forward the enclosed message of sympathy from Their Most Gracious Majesties the King and Queen. I am at the same time to express the regret of the Army Council at the soldier's death in his Country's service.

I am to add that any information that may be received as to the soldier's burial will be communicated to you in due course. A separate leaflet dealing more fully with this subject is enclosed.

I am, your most humble and obedient servant

A reproduction of a notification of the death of a soldier

> How would you feel if you received notification of the death of a loved one in a war? What questions might you want to ask? How might you feel in the following weeks and months?

Commemoration

Almost every city, town and village in Scotland has a war memorial listing the names of the local men who died during the First World War. On Remembrance Sunday, every November, people gather to pay their respects to the men and women who died during the 'war to end all wars'.

After the war had ended it was decided to build a national memorial to commemorate the Scots who died and Edinburgh Castle was chosen as the site. After much argument about what the building should look like, the Scottish National War Memorial was opened on 14 July 1927. The roll of honour for each of the Scottish regiments was placed inside the memorial.

Find out what *Pro Patria* means. Go to your English teacher and find out about a Wilfred Owen poem that uses those words. How does Owen use the words to make a point? How is that different from the message of the words as they are used on the monument? Which do you agree with most: Owen's use of the words or the official memorial use?

A war memorial
in Burgh of
Maxwelltown,
Dumfries

How would the families of dead Scots soldiers feel about a national memorial?

The Scottish National War Memorial at Edinburgh Castle

Activity 1

Summarise this chapter

Draw a spider diagram to help you summarise the information on the impact of the First World War on the home front in Scotland. You might choose to do the planning for this task in pairs or small groups but it would be a good idea to complete the spider diagram on your own in your workbook or work file. This will give you the opportunity to check how well you know the information.

Using a large piece of paper, make notes on the topics listed below:

- propaganda
- the changing role of women
- rationing

- conscription and conscientious objection
- casualties and death
- commemoration.

If you work in threes, one person can read, one person listen and summarise, and one person can write down the information. Swap roles every time you change topic. Make sure you include at least two pieces of information about each topic.

Choose a double page in your workbook or work file and record the information you have researched in a colourful and well-presented spider diagram.

Activity 2

Revolving circle

Choose one of the topics from the previous task to research, and write a paragraph of between 100 and 200 words explaining the impact of the First World War on your chosen topic.

Divide your class into two groups and form each group into a circle. One group makes an inner circle and the other group makes an outer circle. You should face each other; standing opposite another classmate.

Take it in turns to exchange your information with each other for approximately one minute. Give your classmates a red, amber or green rating and at least one suggestion for information they might have included.

The inner circle then rotates clockwise and the outer circle rotates anti-clockwise. The new pair repeats the process.

The rotation continues until you have all had the opportunity to share information with at least two classmates.

Question practice

National 4

Source A is about the impact of the war on women in Scotland. It is by Margaret Morrison, who went to work in a shell factory in the west of Scotland.

SOURCE A

Until then I had worked as a laundry maid on a big estate. Most of us had never worked on machines before. We were given a week's instruction by one of the foremen. After a while they said we could do as well as any of the skilled workmen. Of course we didn't get the same pay. Working in the explosives section could be dangerous. We worked a 12 hour shift, but the pay was good.

1 Explain in your own words what Source A tells us about the impact of the First World War on women.

Success criteria

Include at least one piece of information explaining the impact of the First World War on women in Scotland.

2 State the origin of Source A. This means that you should identify who made the source and when the source was made.

Success criteria

▶ Include at least one factual point regarding the author, timing or purpose of the source.
▶ Explain your points fully.

National 5

1 Describe the effects of the military losses on Scottish society. (4 marks)

Here are some hints to get you started:

▶ casualties
▶ war memorials
▶ Scottish National War Memorial.

Success criteria

▶ You will need to write an introduction sentence that gives a judgement on the question. For example, 'There were many effects of the military losses on Scottish society.'
▶ Four marks are given for four properly described points about four different things.
▶ You can also get 4 marks for giving your answer in developed points: describing a point, then developing this point with additional detail in a separate sentence. This can reduce the amount you have to write. You will need to give two developed points for a 4-mark answer.
▶ Do not list your points together; you will only get 1 mark for this. You need four different sentences.

Source A, about the response to conscription in Scotland, is adapted from *Scottish Popular Politics from Radicalism to Labour* by W. Hamish Fraser (2000).

SOURCE A

When conscription was introduced, the Independent Labour Party protested along with the No Conscription Fellowship [NCF] and the Women's Peace Crusade launched in Glasgow by Helen Crawfurd. The NCF worked to protect the rights of conscientious objectors; offices were founded throughout the UK, including Edinburgh. They contacted objectors, many of whom had been arrested and imprisoned. The NCF often arranged to help at tribunals and courts, not always successfully.

2 Evaluate the usefulness of Source A as evidence of conscription in Scotland. (You may want to comment on what type of source it is, who wrote it, when they wrote it, why they wrote it, what they say or what has been missed out.) (5 marks)

Success criteria

▶ You will need to write an introduction sentence that gives a judgement on the question. For example, 'Source A is quite/very useful as evidence of …'
▶ For every point, you must say whether it makes the source *more* or *less* useful. If you don't do this, you will not get the mark.
▶ Up to 4 marks are given for evaluative comments about the author, type, purpose and timing of the source.
▶ Up to 2 marks are given for evaluative comments on the relevant parts of the source content that you select.
▶ Up to 2 marks are given for evaluative comments relating to points of information missing from the source.

Domestic impact of war: industry and economy

7 What impact did the war have on Scotland's industry and economy?

What is this chapter about?

The war had a large impact on Scotland's heavy industries. Farming and fishing also changed as a result of wartime demands. Although lots of men either volunteered to fight or were conscripted, there were still many men who worked in what became known as reserved occupations. After the war, the Scottish economy faced new problems. New industries were created but these were more usually found in the Midlands and south of England. Scottish industries lost their advantages and the Scottish economy faced serious problems between 1919 and 1928.

By the end of this chapter you should be able to:

▶ Describe the effect the war had on Scotland's economy.
▶ Explain why the Scottish economy faced continuing problems between 1919 and 1928.

How did the war affect Scotland's economy?

The First World War was not just fought between huge armies. The war cost a fortune to fight. It was worked out that to keep every soldier fighting, at least six people had to be working hard back home to provide the food, the weapons, the equipment and all the things an army needed. To win the war, the government created the Ministry of Munitions to organise the economy and to support its armies.

The job of the Ministry of Munitions was to:

▶ run industries like coal, steel making and the railways to make them more efficient
▶ encourage industries to **diversify** and produce different products.

> **GLOSSARY**
> **Diversify** change from making one product to others needed for the war effort

Heavy industry

Before the war, some of Scotland's **heavy industries** such as shipbuilding, iron and steel manufacture, coal mining and textile production were facing problems due to foreign competition and out-dated methods of production. However, during the war these industries did well. They all benefited from wartime demand.

Case study: Fairfield shipyard, Govan, Glasgow

Vast numbers of men and women worked in the shipyards during this period to assist the war effort. In 1913, 7632 men were employed at the yard. Of these, 2332 joined either the army or the navy, with 164 killed during the war.

Between 1914 and 1918, the number employed grew to more than 9000 people, almost 2000 more than at any other period in the yard's history.

After 1915, women were employed in the yard. They mostly acted as semi-skilled workers or labourers. They were often referred to as 'dilutees' as their employment diluted the strict apprenticeship system which governed how many of each type of skilled employee could be trained.

Types of ship built at Fairfield included minesweepers, submarines, destroyers, battleships and armed merchant cruisers. In total, 43 ships were built by the yard for the Royal Navy. The largest ever built was HMS *Renown*, a 27,000-tonne battlecruiser. It measured over 800 feet, carried six 15-inch guns and had a top speed of 32 knots. This ship was constructed in only 20 months – a record for such a ship at the time.

What is important to remember is that this was only one of many Clyde yards building for the Ministry of Munitions. It is estimated that 43 per cent of the tonnage of ships ordered by the **Admiralty** between 1914 and 1919 was built in the Clyde yards.

Many of the jobs in heavy industry were very skilled and offered good wages to the men doing them. These jobs were **reserved occupations**, meaning they were so important to the war effort that these workers were not allowed to join the armed forces. For example, a skilled engineer making engines for ships or an experienced coal miner producing fuel were of much greater use to the war effort than as soldiers going over the top on the front line.

Reserved occupations also included drivers of trains or workers in munitions factories. Some men worked as farmers, who were needed to grow food for the troops and civilians. Other men guarded the coast in case of an enemy invasion. These skilled men were not allowed to volunteer for the fighting and were exempt from conscription.

Many clergymen also stayed at home to look after the pastoral needs of their parishes (communities) though some went to war as chaplains to look after the fighting men. Doctors were needed to tend the sick and wounded at home in Britain and at the front too.

War materials

Engineering firms also benefited. Beardmore's engineering firm, based in Parkhead, expanded to employ 20,000 men at its sites. It built aircraft, artillery pieces, tanks and even airships.

Ammunition production led to a doubling of steel output. This industry employed 24,000 men in the Clyde Valley.

In Edinburgh, there was an expansion of the North British Rubber Company to meet demand for gas masks, waterproof coats, boots and sheets.

> ## GLOSSARY
>
> **Heavy industry** industries such as coal mining and steel making
>
> **Admiralty** the government department that ran the Royal Navy
>
> **Reserved occupations** vital wartime jobs done by skilled men who could not be conscripted

In Dundee, the jute industry expanded to produce jute sacks for sandbags and nosebags for horses. At one point, the army needed six million jute bags per month. This demand led to large profits and also high wages for the workers in this industry.

Demand for steel saw a huge rise in output. By 1918, Glasgow steelworks were producing 90 per cent of Britain's armour plate, used for warships and tanks.

In textile (cloth) production, factories rushed to meet army demands for uniforms and canvas materials for tents for the men on the Western Front.

Farming and fishing

Shepherds were in demand because their sheep produced the wool for military uniforms. In 1916, the government bought every bit of wool cut from sheep, and wages for shepherds almost doubled to £2 per week by the end of the war.

In farming, wages doubled for most farm workers during the war. Although many farms lost their labourers as the men left for the armed forces, older men, boys and women took their places and production of food increased during the war. Farm owners were encouraged to keep up production by the government, which paid guaranteed prices for farm products such as potatoes and milk.

However, it was not all good news. The fishing industry declined as the North Sea was closed to fishing. Even on the west coast, fishermen were restricted to the waters close to shore because of the threat posed by German submarines and surface ships. The huge pre-war market for herring in Russia, Poland and even Germany was lost because of the war. The number of fishermen dropped and the amount of cod and haddock caught fell from 1.5 million tonnes to 0.5 million tonnes in 1917. As a result, fish had to be rationed.

Although the war created an impression of busy and profitable industries in Scotland, it was false. The profits from wartime increases in production would not last when the war ended. The war created an artificial boom in industry but this merely hid the reality that Scotland's industries had been in decline before 1914.

What happened to Scotland's economy after the war?

The Scottish economy did well out of the war. However, it struggled in the years of peace that followed. The trouble was that heavy industry, which Scotland was good at, was no longer in demand. The new industries such as car making, chemicals and electrical goods were being set up elsewhere.

Another change in Scotland's economy was that new machines were doing the work that previously was done by well-paid, skilled workers. Now, the same work could be done by lower-paid, semi-skilled and even unskilled workers using the new technology.

Finally, while Scotland had focused its industrial production during the war on winning the war, other countries such as India and the USA were developing their own industries. Foreign competition was one reason why Britain's share of world trade in manufacturing fell from 30 per cent in 1913 to 22 per cent in 1929.

Assume the soldier is the same man who appears with the woman and baby. How do you think he felt in 1923? Spidergram as many words as you can that could apply to both the man and the woman. What sort of organisation would produce this poster? Give reasons for your answers.

'Yesterday – the trenches. To-day – unemployed.' These posters were produced in 1923 and summed up how many ex-soldiers felt in Scotland in the 1920s.

How was shipbuilding affected after the war?

Between 1921 and 1923, shipping built on the Clyde fell from 510,000 to 170,000 tonnes. Shipyards closed as orders dried up. Why was there such a fall in demand?

▶ Scottish shipyards had to depend on orders from the Admiralty. These orders for new ships ended when the war finished.

▶ Foreign shipyards were more efficient than the Scottish ones.

▶ In smaller boat-building yards up and down the coast, fewer fishing vessels were being built as export markets in eastern Europe were lost.

How was railway engine production affected?

Locomotive (railway engine) production fell by two-thirds at the North British Locomotive Company. Engineering work declined as companies **amalgamated**. Their headquarters moved from Scotland to London.

What happened to coal production?

In 1913, Scottish coal fields had produced 42.5 million tonnes of coal. By 1926, this had fallen to 16.8 million tonnes. Scottish coal was difficult to get out of the ground and that made it expensive to produce. Alternative fuels such as oil meant a fall in demand for coal. Wage cuts led to strikes by the miners and Scotland gained a reputation as a troublesome place to do business. This led to a lack of investment by other businesses.

How did the end of the war affect the jute industry?

Quite simply, the orders from the army for jute sacks stopped. There was also competition from India. Jute is a fibre that was brought from Bangladesh (then part of India) to Dundee and made into a very hard-wearing cloth. During and after the war, India started building its own jute mills.

What happened to farming?

Government **subsidies** for farmers finished in 1920. World prices fell by at least 25 per cent during this period. New machines increased output but needed fewer workers, so fewer jobs were available.

Did the government try to help the industries that were facing such problems?

Yes, it did. The government organised a conference in Ottawa, Canada, to encourage trade with the empire and Commonwealth.

Marketing boards were set up to help producers of milk, eggs, potatoes and bacon. These boards paid guaranteed prices for products.

Taxes were put on foreign imports which made Scottish products more competitively priced.

Scottish farmers also changed their usual habits and started growing new produce such as poultry, soft fruit and vegetables.

Companies were encouraged to scrap old machinery and to work together to reduce costs and increase production. In Scotland, these included the railways and steel industries.

The government set up the Department of Scientific and Industrial Research to develop new industries such as petrochemicals and aviation.

What new industrial changes took place in the 1920s?

New industries such as those making electrical goods, chemical engineering and car assembly were based on mass production and mass consumption.

The old, heavy industries were built near coal fields, iron ore supplies and deep rivers because raw materials needed

> Look at both posters advertising consumer goods. How relevant would these new consumer goods be to a population facing economic depression and unemployment?

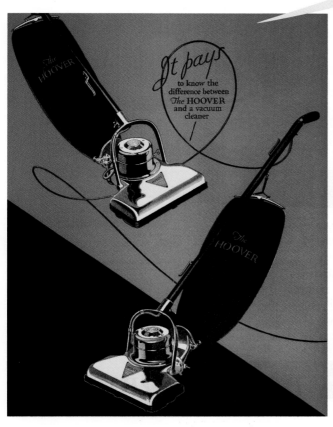

A vacuum cleaner advertisement

A car advertisement

for production were expensive to transport. The new industries did not have to worry about raw materials needed for production. Their factories were powered by electricity and were built near their new customers, usually in central and southern England.

Electricity also powered the new products such as electric irons, vacuum cleaners and so on. Advertisements encouraged people to buy these products with the promise of giving them more time for leisure activities.

Why did the new industries not really help Scotland?

The problem Scotland faced was that many areas were not connected to the national electrical grid. In 1938, over 700,000 people (40 per cent of the population) were still without an electricity supply.

Scotland's population was small and unemployment meant that people could not afford the new products. Therefore, the growing industries tended to stay in the south of Britain. Scotland did not attract enough of these growing industries to offset the problems which the older industries had experienced.

Activity 1

Summarise this chapter

Take a whole page in your workbook or work file. Write the title 'Who were the winners and losers of Scottish industry during the First World War?'

Now draw up a table with three columns headed 'Winners', 'Losers' and 'Reasons'. Place each Scottish industry in either the 'Winners' or 'Losers' column. For each industry, find at least one piece of information to support your answer and write it down in the 'Reasons' column.

Make sure you record information on all of the following industries:

▶ agriculture
▶ fishing
▶ shipbuilding
▶ engineering
▶ textiles
▶ coal mining
▶ steel making.

Activity 2

Take a large piece of paper. Draw the outline of a factory with a chimney.
Divide the inside of the factory into seven sections. These have to be quite large. Each section represents one of the main industries in Scotland.

Within each section, note down the problems that industry faced after the war and why they happened. Make sure that you include at least two pieces of relevant information for each industry. Draw a small diagram/picture to identify each industry.

Make sure you include all the main industries (listed above in Activity 1).

Activity 3

'Walk around, talk around'

Work in pairs or in small groups. Take a large piece of paper and draw a triangle that fills most of the page.

Your teacher will allocate a period of time. Fill the triangle with as much information as you can on how the First World War affected Scottish industry. Once your time is up, leave your paper and move on to the next group's paper.

Your teacher will allocate another period of time. Add more information to the new group's paper outside the triangle. Keep moving round until all the information is on the paper or the paper is filled.

As a class, discuss and confirm that all the main points of information about the short- and long-term impacts of the war on Scottish industry have been included on each group's paper.

All of the class should take part in discussing and recording information.

Question practice

National 4

Source A is about the impact of the war on Scottish industry and economy.

SOURCE A

The First World War changed Scottish industry and economy. During the war, Scottish industries did well because Scotland was good at making products which the military needed, such as ships. After the war, Scottish industry suffered from increased foreign competition. Scotland did not develop new industries as fast as it needed to.

1 Describe the impact of the First World War on Scottish industry. You should use Source A and your own knowledge.

Success criteria

Include at least two points or one developed piece of information about the impact of the First World War on Scottish industry.

Source B is about the impact of the war on Scottish industry. It is from *The Flowers of the Forest: Scotland and the First World War* by historian Trevor Royle and was published in 2007.

SOURCE B

During the war, Scotland fully justified its title of the workshop of the war. However, the profits disguised the fact that most industries had been in decline before 1914. The boom years during the war became a distant memory as the world economy slumped in the 1920s.

2 State the origin of Source B. This means that you should identify who wrote the source and when the source was written.

Success criteria

▸ Include at least one factual point regarding the author, timing or purpose of the source.
▸ Explain your points fully.

National 5

1 Describe the impact of the First World War on Scottish farming and fishing industries. (4 marks)

Here are some hints to get you started:

- The fishing industry declined as the North Sea was closed to fishing.
- Limited fishing was possible on the west coast. Fishermen were able to fish inland waters.
- The numbers of fishermen dropped from 32,678 to 21,870 by 1917.
- The amount of white fish caught dropped from 1.5 million tonnes in 1914 to 0.5 million tonnes in 1917.
- Fish became rationed as a result of the war.
- Agriculture in Scotland benefited through sheep farming.
- Wool was in demand for military uniforms.
- Wages for shepherds doubled from £1 to £2 a week.
- There was an increase in crops, such as oats, being grown.

Success criteria

- You will need to write an introduction sentence that gives a judgement on the question. For example, 'There were many effects of the First World War on Scottish farming and industry.'
- Four marks are given for four properly described points about four different things.
- You can also get 4 marks for giving your answer in developed points: describing a point, then developing this point with additional detail in a separate sentence. This can reduce the amount you have to write. You will need to give two developed points for a 4-mark answer.
- Do not list your points together; you will only get 1 mark for this. You need four different sentences.

Source A is about the impact of the First World War on the Scottish economy.

SOURCE A

During the war, production techniques had improved. Skilled workers had been replaced by semi-skilled and even unskilled workers. After the war, there was an economic boom but this did not last in the 1920s. At the end of the war, there was a drop in demand for the goods that Scotland produced. There was reduced need for battleships, for example.

2 How fully does Source A show the impact of the First World War on the Scottish economy? Use Source A and recall to reach a judgement. (6 marks)

This is a 'how fully' question. In this type of question you need to select the points from the source which are relevant to the question – usually there will be three points in the source. Then, to get full marks, you need to bring in points from recall that are also relevant to the question.

Success criteria

▶ You will need to write an introduction sentence that gives a judgement on the question. For example, 'Source A does not fully explain the impact of the First World War on the Scottish economy.'
▶ A maximum of 2 marks may be given for answers in which no judgement has been made.
▶ Up to 3 marks can be gained for explaining pieces of information from the source.
▶ Up to 4 marks can be gained for explaining pieces of information from your own knowledge which are relevant to the question asked.
▶ Pieces of information from your own knowledge can act either as further explanation of pieces of information from the source or as new points.

3 How important was the shipbuilding industry to the Scottish war effort during the First World War? (9 marks)

Planning your answer:

▶ In small groups or pairs, create a spidergram containing information on the importance of the shipbuilding industry and other factors to the war effort. Other factors might include: jute and textiles, farming and fishing.
▶ Find at least two facts per paragraph.
▶ Plan an overall response to the question.
▶ Show your plan to your teacher before starting your first draft.
▶ Read through your work carefully and mark any mistakes you spot with a green pen, then correct your work before handing it to your teacher.
▶ Rewrite the final draft of your answer.

Success criteria

▶ One mark is available for an introduction, which should contain background and factors that you are going to write about.
▶ One mark is available for balance in your answer. This means you will have to mention at least two factors about the importance of Scottish industry to the war effort during the First World War. That means at least two paragraphs of writing.
▶ This sort of question has a factor in it; in this case, it is shipbuilding. You should discuss this factor first in your answer.
▶ Five marks are available for the relevant and detailed knowledge points that you are going to explain in your answer.
▶ Two marks are available for your conclusion. One mark is given for a judgement and one mark is given for a supporting reason for your conclusion.

4 Explain the reasons Scottish industry declined after the First World War (6 marks)

Here are some hints to get you started:

▶ The artificial boom caused by the First World War.
▶ There was a worldwide slump in trade.
▶ There was also increasing foreign competition.
▶ The impact of the war on shipbuilding and engineering.
▶ The increasing use of machines.
▶ The impact of the war on jute and agriculture.

Success criteria

▶ You will need to write an introduction sentence that answers the question. For example: 'There are many reasons why Scottish industry declined after the First World War.'
▶ You must give six reasons or three developed points explaining why Scottish industry declined after the First World War.

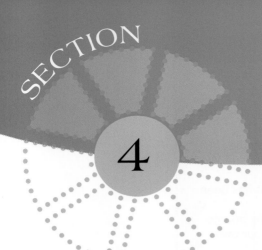

SECTION

4

Domestic impact of war: politics

8 What effects did the war have on the role of women?

What is this chapter about?

The role of women changed greatly as a result of their wartime experiences. Many women found themselves in employment which had previously been described as men's work. Others had been radicalised by the war, which meant they had decided to take action themselves against things they felt were unfair. In 1918, some women were given the right to vote. However, the government's wartime promises of the creation of 'homes fit for heroes' were to prove impossible to achieve and the new opportunities that had opened for women during the war rapidly closed again when the war ended.

By the end of this chapter you should be able to:

▸ Describe what women did during the war.
▸ Explain in what ways attitudes towards women changed during the war.
▸ Describe the problems facing Scottish women after the war.

The roles of men and women in British society

In 1900, women did not have social equality with men. One important difference was the right to vote in elections. By 1900, six men out of ten could vote in general elections. Women could not. Why was this?

Why could women not vote in national elections?

The short answer is that the male-dominated society did not think women were equal to men. During the nineteenth century, many people thought that a woman's place was at home. Many also believed that women were too emotional to vote or that their husbands would easily influence them. However, things were changing.

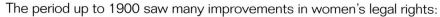

The period up to 1900 saw many improvements in women's legal rights:

▶ By 1900, women could vote in elections to school boards. The first woman to be elected in Scotland was Miss Jane Arthur to the Paisley School Board in 1873.
▶ Women could vote in local elections if they paid rates – a sort of local tax.
▶ Women could now divorce their husbands and yet retain access to their children.
▶ When women married they could now keep their own money and property. Until 1882, women had to give all their money and possessions to their husbands when they married.

At work, women faced a lot of unfair treatment. For a start, women were not paid the same as men for doing the same job. In 1900, it is estimated that women were paid 40 per cent less than men. In many careers, like teaching, women also had to give up their job when they married.

Education for girls seemed to be well established by 1900. Since 1872, Scotland's boys and girls had to go to primary school and, by 1914, they had to stay at school until they were 14 years of age. However, girls were treated differently from boys. Girls usually had to study needlework, cookery and laundry. In 1910, care of infants was added to their curriculum. This was to prepare girls for their role as homemakers.

At university level, women faced even more problems. They could only go to universities in 1889 when the Universities (Scotland) Act gave them access on the same basis as men. This allowed some women to become doctors, teachers and lawyers. However, male attitudes were still hostile and university education was expensive.

Why did women want the vote?

Many women believed they could end the unfairness of society and be treated as equal human beings only if they had the right to vote. Women wanted to be able to choose who ran the country and to make sure laws were passed to help women gain equality with men. As historian Elspeth King wrote:

Allowing women to vote would free them from low pay, poor working conditions, domestic violence and prostitution. It was also the key to obtaining better education for women and, in particular, medical education which would enable them to become doctors and therefore be able to help other women.

How did women campaign for the right to vote?

During the mid-nineteenth century, local organisations were set up to fight for the right of women to vote. They were called **suffrage** societies. In 1897, the National Union of Women's Suffrage Societies (NUWSS) brought all these local organisations together into a national organisation. The NUWSS had widespread support and its members became known as suffragists.

GLOSSARY
Suffrage right to vote

The leader of the suffragists was Mrs Millicent Fawcett. She felt that it was unfair that women paid taxes, obeyed the law and could vote in local and school board elections, yet they were not trusted to vote in national elections.

In 1902, the Glasgow and West of Scotland Association for Women's Suffrage was formed. It joined the NUWSS in October 1903. Similar organisations appeared in Dundee and Aberdeen. In 1909, all these suffrage societies came together under the Scottish Federation of Women's Suffrage Societies, which was itself a part of the NUWSS.

The poster below tries to show why it was unfair that highly skilled women could not vote while many lesser-skilled men could vote. Nowadays this poster would be considered not politically correct because it seems to suggest that a person with disabilities should not vote because he could not fight for his country. The poster also describes one man as being a proprietor of white slaves. This meant he controlled prostitutes and lived off their earnings – and yet was still allowed to vote.

Discuss with your classmates and decide if you agree with the argument made in this poster to win women the vote. What do you like and dislike about this poster? Does it work?

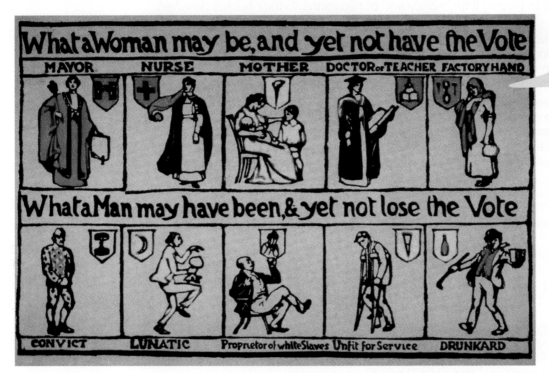

An example of suffragist propaganda

How successful were the suffragists?

The suffragists wanted votes for women. They believed that this should be achieved by peaceful, lawful methods. Suffragist methods included leaflet and poster campaigns and presenting signed petitions to parliament. Between 1867 and 1876, two million signatures were obtained in Scotland for petitions in favour of granting women the vote. To spread its ideas further, the NUWSS also set up its own newspaper, *The Common Cause*.

The support given to the NUWSS can be seen in the fact that by 1914 the NUWSS had over 500 branches and 100,000 members. Candidates standing for election and who supported votes for women were helped by NUWSS members. The NUWSS also supported the Labour Party as it wanted the vote for all men and women. These peaceful methods helped to convince many Liberal and Conservative Party members that women deserved the vote.

However, there was frustration among many women about the lack of progress. This led to the formation of a more radical organisation demanding votes for women.

Who were the suffragettes?

In Manchester in 1903, Mrs Emmeline Pankhurst, with the help of her daughters, Christabel and Sylvia, set up the Women's Social and Political Union (WSPU). Supporters of the WSPU were called suffragettes by the *Daily Mail* newspaper.

The motto of this organisation was 'Deeds not words'. This showed that the members were unhappy with the methods of the suffragists. Sylvia said the NUWSS was 'so staid, so willing to wait, so leisurely'. She meant that they were too polite, too slow and seemed to be getting nowhere.

What were the aims of the suffragettes?

The suffragettes' aim was, like the suffragists, to obtain the vote in national elections for women. However, they were prepared to break the law to achieve their aim. The suffragettes believed that the campaign of the NUWSS had been a failure. Christabel Pankhurst believed the WSPU was fighting a war. To win this war, total loyalty and obedience were demanded. Such hard-line tactics created tensions within the organisation.

What methods did the suffragettes use?

Suffragettes were no longer prepared to wait to get the vote; they would demand it. This policy is called **militancy**, and it created a lot of publicity for the movement. They produced posters and pamphlets and held demonstrations.

GLOSSARY

Militancy aggressive or warring activity

At first, the suffragettes would heckle speakers at political meetings and they held demonstrations outside the Houses of Parliament. This often led to their arrest for a breach of the peace. These demonstrations included spitting at a policeman or chaining themselves to the railings outside parliament. As time went on, their tactics became more extreme. Buildings were set on fire, bomb attacks were made on properties and famous paintings in art galleries were slashed.

What did the suffragettes do in Scotland?

The leader of the Scottish suffragettes was Flora Drummond. She was known as 'The General' because of her organisational abilities and because she always wore military-style uniforms. She organised all of the great suffragette demonstrations, such as the one in Princes Street, Edinburgh, in 1909.

In 1906, the first branch of the WSPU opened in Glasgow. Its headquarters, in Bath Street, opened two years later. At first they held public meetings, raised funds through book sales and opened more branches across Scotland.

In 1909, the first militant demonstrations were held in Glasgow and Dundee when women tried to force their way into political meetings. By 1913, their campaign was more violent. Acid was poured into pillar boxes to destroy letters and attacks on property also increased. Telegraph and telephone wires were cut. There was an attempt to blow up the cottage in Alloway where Robert Burns had been born. There was also an attempt to burn down the grandstand at Kelso racecourse.

Suffragettes march down Princes Street in Edinburgh, led by Flora Drummond and Emmeline Pankhurst in 1909

Are street demonstrations and processions effective for campaign groups trying to create change? Think about protests such as the suffragettes' and campaigns nowadays. How would you choose to protest or demonstrate? Be prepared to explain your choice.

On 29 August 1913, the *Glasgow Herald* reported the following 'suffragette outrage':

Struggle on the Golf Links

About half past five, when Mr Asquith [the Prime Minister] reached the seventeenth green, two women suddenly appeared at the scene. They seized hold of the Prime Minister and began to drag him about, and in the struggle Mr Asquith's hat was knocked off. Mr Asquith's daughter called for assistance and in a few seconds two private detectives, who accompany Mr Asquith, arrived on the scene and dragged the women away.

The most notorious suffragette protest took place in 1913 at a famous horse race called the Derby, in which a horse owned by King George V was running. A suffragette called Emily Wilding Davison tried to stop the king's horse to draw attention to the cause of votes for women. Emily was knocked over by the galloping racehorse and she died of her injuries a few days later. Emily's funeral was turned into a huge publicity event by fellow suffragettes who claimed she was a martyr for the cause of women's suffrage.

Not all women, or even all suffragettes, supported the violent campaign. This led to a split in the WSPU in 1907 and the set-up of the Women's Freedom League. This had many supporters in Scotland. The Women's Freedom League did not believe in violence but was still prepared to break the law to achieve its aim. This included refusing to pay tax to the government.

The collision between the racehorse and Emily Davison in 1913. A film of the event can be found on YouTube™

Do you think Emily Davison really was a martyr? Do some research to find out what other opinions there are about her. For example, why did she have a return rail ticket in her bag? Did she mean to get trampled?

How did people react to suffragette tactics?

Suffragettes were reported in most newspapers as irresponsible law-breakers who did not deserve the right to vote. They were described as women who neglected their families. Male supporters of female suffrage were portrayed as hen-pecked husbands.

Nonetheless, male supporters of female suffrage eventually set up the Men's League for Women's Suffrage.

Thousands of women left the suffragettes and joined the suffragists, who continued to believe in persuading people that women should have the vote. Support came from local town councils and from Scottish churches. Town councils passed motions in support of women's suffrage. In July 1912, the Scottish Churches League for Women's Suffrage was set up.

Why do you think the woman is portrayed in this way?

An anti-suffragette poster

How did the government react to suffragette actions?

To attract publicity, women were prepared to break the law. However, in July 1909, the suffragette Marion Wallace Dunlop created a sensation when she went on hunger strike in protest at her imprisonment. After 91 hours without food she was released. Other arrested suffragettes now followed her example. The government could not allow people to break the law and then be seen to get away with it. So, in September 1909, the Home Secretary decided that prisoners on hunger strike should be fed forcibly.

Many people were horrified by such treatment. The most shocking treatment of women was in Perth prison, where experiments were carried out to see if rectal feeding was possible in an attempt to get liquid into the woman's body. The suffragettes reacted by producing posters that claimed women were being tortured.

Force-feeding of women made the government very unpopular and politicians worried about what would happen if a hunger striker died in prison. As a result, the government passed a new law called the Prisoner's Temporary Discharge (for ill health) Act in 1913. Under this Act, prisoners on hunger strike were released when they were very weak. Once they were at home and healthy again, they would be re-arrested. The suffragettes called this the Cat and Mouse Act as they felt the government was playing with prisoners in the way that a cat plays with a mouse.

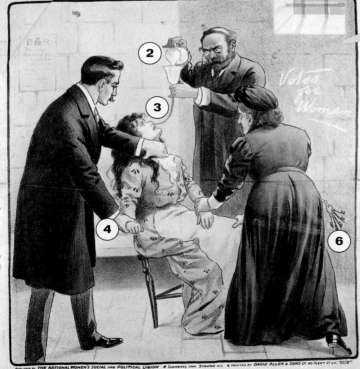

Explain what each number is showing and then explain the purpose of this poster. Would it be effective in achieving its purpose?

A poster showing a woman in prison being force-fed liquid using a tube inserted through one nostril

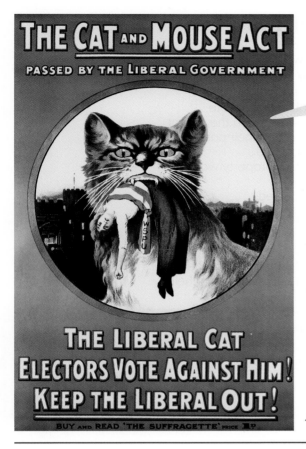

Describe in detail everything that you see in this poster. Why did the artist choose to include all these things? How useful is this in helping you to reach an informed and balanced view about the suffragette campaign before 1914?

A poster protesting against the Cat and Mouse Act

How did attitudes to women and the vote change during the Great War?

With the outbreak of war in 1914, many suffragettes ended their campaign for votes for women.

In August 1914, writing in *The Common Cause*, Mrs Fawcett declared:

Women, your country needs you. We have another duty now. Let us show ourselves worthy of citizenship, whether our claim to it be recognised or not.

Attitudes to women changed in consequence of women's war work. The results of this work were highlighted by Prime Minister Asquith during the early part of the war. He had previously been strongly against votes for women, but by the end of the war he said:

How could we have carried on the war without them? I find it impossible to withhold from women the power and the right of making their voices directly heard.

The extension of the franchise

By 1916, the attitude of the government towards votes for women had changed. It was clear that extending the **franchise** to women was only a matter of time. This was due to a number of factors.

▶ The pre-war militant tactics had been a barrier to the granting of the vote.
▶ The truce, declared on the outbreak of war in August 1914, stopped the violent attacks and so led the way to many former opponents changing their position.
▶ Fears concerning a female majority at election time were calmed.
▶ Concerns among Scottish socialists that women who owned property would support the Conservative Party were reduced.
▶ The contribution of women to the war effort could not be denied.

By 1918, even Asquith had changed his mind about votes for women and in that year the Representation of the People Act was passed. Its terms included:

▶ that all men over the age of 21 were given the vote
▶ that women over 30 who owned their own homes or were married to householders were given the vote. Women who were university graduates could vote in their university city.

Despite adding six million men and two million women to the British **electorate**, this Act still discriminated against women. Almost all working-class women still could not vote.

The first female MP to take her seat in parliament was Nancy Astor, who was elected in December 1919. By 1931, there were 15 female MPs.

Finally, in 1928, the right to vote was given to all men and women over the age of 21.

The fight for women's suffrage had been won.

GLOSSARY

Franchise the right to vote in public elections

Electorate people who have the right to vote in an election

What other action did Scottish women take during the war?

The war had a dramatic impact on the economy of Scotland. Thousands of workers had flocked to Glasgow and other towns in the west of Scotland to find work in the war industries. This had led to a shortage of housing. Landlords tried to exploit this situation by increasing rents. This resulted in social unrest and direct action in Glasgow, which then spread to other areas. As many men were away fighting, the landlords thought that the women would be a soft touch. Instead, women got angry and took direct action. Women were already campaigning against the poor maintenance of their dwellings and the greed of the landlords in failing to carry out repairs.

How are the protestors trying to justify the rent strike as the right thing to do during the war?

The 1915 rent strikes in Glasgow. To understand all of the posters you need to know that Prussians were Germans, from the state of Prussia in Germany. Partick is an area of Glasgow.

What were the rent strikes?

The rent strikes were protests about the high cost of housing in Glasgow, Dundee and Aberdeen. They mainly happened during 1915.

Many existing tenants could not afford the new higher costs. Landlords then tried to evict these tenants. At the same time, the price of food and fuel was also increasing.

It was mostly women who had to cope with these price increases as their men were away fighting in the war. These women resented the fact that landlords were trying to exploit the war for their own profit. Resentment increased and resistance to evictions grew. Resistance was organised like this: one woman with a bell would sit in the tenement close, watching while the other women living in the tenement

A rent strike poster issued by the Glasgow Labour Party Housing Association, 1915. The poster comes with instructions to tack it 'to top of lower sash'. That means stick the poster in your window!

went on with their household duties. Whenever the bailiff's officer appeared to evict a tenant, the woman in the passage immediately rang the bell and the other women put down whatever work they were doing and hurried to where the alarm was being raised. They would hurl flour bombs and other missiles at the bailiff, forcing him to make a hasty retreat. It is said that they even pulled down his trousers to humiliate him!

On 16 February 1915, the Glasgow Women's Housing Association was set up, led by Helen Crawfurd, Mary Barbour, Agnes Dollan and Jessie Stephens. Its aim was to protect tenants against rent increases. It did this by encouraging tenants to join together and to resist rent rises.

Mary Barbour, the wife of a Fairfield shipyard worker, was involved in every aspect of activities from organising committees to preventing evictions and hounding the sheriff's officers:

Mary Barbour

In Govan, on one occasion, a woman had been persuaded by the House Factor to pay the increase. She had been told that the other tenants had paid; Mrs Barbour got the men from the shipyards in Govan to come out onto the street where the House Factor's office was. They all went up with the woman and demanded a return of the money. On the Factor being shown the thousands of black-faced workers crowding the streets, he handed it over.

What happened during the rent strikes?

The first real test came in May 1915 in South Govan in Glasgow. Large meetings were held to support those who refused to pay the increased rents. These women were not against the war but were opposed to landlords making money from the situation.

The protests were organised very efficiently. The women accused landlords of being unpatriotic. They were also supported by the employers as they did not want to see industrial production affected.

When law officers were sent to evict tenants for not paying, supporters of the rent strikes made it impossible for these officers to carry out the evictions. By the end of 1915, 25,000 tenants had joined the movement.

On 17 November 1915, the trial was due to take place of 18 tenants who had refused to pay increased rents. There was a huge meeting in George Square, Glasgow, to show opposition to the trial. Factory owners were worried when men went on unofficial strike to show their support for the people on trial.

Joseph Melling, a historian of the rent strikes, commented on the importance of the way in which the industrial and housing protests combined to challenge the authority of landlords and the state. Another historian, James Smyth, considered that:

It may well have been the most successful example of direct action ever undertaken by the Scottish working class.

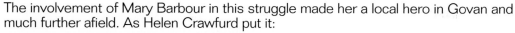

The involvement of Mary Barbour in this struggle made her a local hero in Govan and much further afield. As Helen Crawfurd put it:

This struggle brought great masses of women together.

Mary was the first female Baillie of the City of Glasgow Corporation and one of the first female magistrates.

What did the government do about the rent strikes?

The government response was swift. The Rent Restriction Act was rushed through parliament, which froze rents at their pre-war levels. Increases were only allowed if improvements had been made to the property. It was a victory for direct action.

The people's action in the short term had solved the situation. The long-term consequence of the rent strikes was that many more people came to take an interest in politics.

In which other political areas did women become involved?

Some of these radical females also became involved in other political areas. Helen Crawfurd, one of the leaders of the rent strikes, launched the Women's Peace Crusade on 10 June 1916. This was the first attempt to organise people in all social classes to oppose the war. There were branches across Scotland and on 8 July 1917, over 14,000 protesters gathered on Glasgow Green. Other organisations included the Women's International League for Peace and Freedom. This was set up by Chrystal Macmillan, who was a graduate of Edinburgh University.

'Homes fit for heroes'

As the war neared its end, the government promised the people that life would be better after the war. In other words, the government tried to convince voters that the war had been worth fighting. One thing that was promised was 'homes fit for heroes'. In 1918, the Prime Minister Lloyd George said:

What is our task? To make Britain a fit country for heroes to live in. That is our first task. One of the ways of dealing with that is, of course, to deal with the housing conditions. Slums are not fit homes for the men who have won this war, or their children. The housing of the people must be a national concern.

The government knew that a lot of the housing across Scotland was shockingly bad. The 1917 Royal Commission, which investigated the state of housing in Scotland, found:

▶ huge overcrowding in houses
▶ a lack of basic sanitary services such as toilets in many villages and towns
▶ an unacceptable number of one-roomed houses occupied by large families
▶ a lack of proper light and ventilation in homes.

In the years after the Great War, the government did try to improve housing but its efforts were not particularly significant.

Addison's Act (1919)

This Act was passed to make good on the promise of 'homes fit for heroes'. The money ran out in 1921.

Local councils were given subsidies from central government to build cheap rented houses. By 1922, 312,000 homes were built. However, poor families could not afford to pay the rents for these houses.

An example of the type of housing built under this Act can be found at Riddrie. It was the first housing scheme built for the Glasgow Corporation in an attempt to meet the estimated need for 57,000 new houses in the aftermath of the First World War.

The Riddrie scheme was built between 1920 and 1927, and included a mixture of semi-detached and terraced cottages with gardens and three-storey tenement flats. All the houses had cavity walling and electric servicing, something new at the time. Around 1000 houses were built, most of them allocated to skilled workers earning above-average wages.

Wheatley Housing Act (1924)

John Wheatley

John Wheatley was an MP and Cabinet Minister. During the First World War he became one of the leading figures in the Independent Labour Party. He won the Shettleston seat in Glasgow for the ILP in 1922 and held it until his death in 1930.

Wheatley's great interest was in working-class housing and he fought for good quality public-sector housing to replace city slums. Wheatley promoted the 1924 Housing Act as Minister of Health in the first Labour government, developing a partnership between political parties, local authorities and specially appointed committees of building employees and employers, to build large numbers of new **council houses** at modest rents. These houses were built with electricity, gardens and indoor toilets. Central government gave subsidies to local councils to build houses.

By 1933, 500,000 council houses had been built. Once again, poor families could not afford to pay the rents for these houses.

Despite these improvements, Scottish housing remained poor. The Scots were unforgiving, blaming the Liberals for the failure to deliver on their promises.

> **GLOSSARY**
>
> **Council houses** homes built by local authorities for local people to rent

Identify and list the difficulties and dangers of living in sub-standard housing conditions such as these.

A 'home fit for a hero'? An ex-soldier and his family living in a canvas hut in the 1920s.

Activity 1

True or false?

Work with a partner and together decide whether each of the statements below is true or false.

Then copy the statements into your workbook or work file and, next to each one, give a reason why the statement is true or false.

▶ Women did not get the vote in 1918.
▶ The surge in war industry in Scotland led to housing problems and rent strikes.
▶ Women rent strikers did not get much support.
▶ The government moved quickly to address the concerns of the strikers.
▶ The government did a lot to try to deal with housing problems after the war.
▶ More people got the right to vote in 1918.

Activity 2

As a journalist, you have been asked to investigate and report on the political changes that have happened in Scotland as a result of the First World War. Think about what sort of questions you might want answered. To help get you started, use the following hints:

▶ What happened to the women's campaign for the vote when war broke out?
▶ What evidence is there that attitudes to women changed as a result of the First World War?
▶ Why did the First World War cause women to get involved in rent strikes?
▶ How successful were the rent strikes?
▶ How successful were the efforts to improve housing in Scotland after the First World War?

Write these questions down in your workbook or work file and add your own. Find evidence to answer these questions and note your answers in your workbook or work file.

Now you can plan your article. Make notes and structure what you are going to write in your report. Write your first draft of your article.

Read through your work carefully and mark any mistakes you spot with a green pen, then correct your work before handing it to your teacher.

Ensure that information which answers all the questions can be found in your article. Your article should be structured and well organised.

Activity 3

In your workbook or work file, write down the questions you would like answered about how the First World War changed attitudes to women and their political activity in Scotland. You should try to think of at least three questions.

Dedicate a wall space for a 'No easy answers' board in the classroom. Hold a class discussion on whether your questions have been answered and agree on which questions should go on the classroom's 'No easy answers' board.

At various points during the course of the topic, revisit the ideas and questions on the board to see if your understanding has developed.

Question practice

National 4

Source A is about the changes in attitudes to women as a result of the First World War.

SOURCE A

The First World War brought a change to the jobs women did. Women replaced men who had left their jobs to join the forces and also worked in the new munitions factories that sprang up. This led to women gaining more confidence. Politicians and leaders were very impressed with the war work done by women and wanted to give them the vote.

1 Explain why the First World War led to women getting the vote. You should use Source A and your own knowledge.

Success criteria

Include at least one piece of information explaining how the First World War led to women getting the vote.

Sources B and C are about the rent strikes in Glasgow.

SOURCE B

The first direct action taken was to not pay the rent increases. It was taken by women in Govan, Glasgow. When rent was not paid, sheriff's officers moved in to remove the tenants who had not paid. Protestors, on hearing of these evictions, made it impossible for the sheriff's officers to carry out their evictions. They did this by flooding the streets with protestors.

SOURCE C

The protests were organised by women very effectively. They accused landlords of being anti-patriotic and refused to pay rent. Women worked to stop sheriff officers evicting tenants. Crowds gathered in support of tenants who were due in court for refusing to pay rent increases.

2 Compare the views in Sources B and C about the rent strikes. Describe in detail their similarities and/or differences. You can also briefly compare the overall attitude of the sources.

Success criteria

‣ Examine the two sources in order to show two simple points of comparison or one developed point of similarity or difference.
‣ A simple comparison: 'Source B says … and Source C says …'.
‣ A developed comparison: 'Sources B and C agree about the women leading the rent strikes. Source B says … and Source C says …'.

National 5

1 Explain the reasons why the First World War increased women's involvement in politics. (6 marks)

Here are some hints to get you started:

- the impact of the war on the campaign for votes for women
- the role of women in resisting rent increases
- the activities of women during the rent strikes
- victory for women in the rent strikes.

Success criteria

- You will need to write an introduction sentence that answers the question. For example, 'There are many reasons why the First World War increased women's involvement in politics'.
- You must give six reasons or three developed points explaining why the First World War led to increased women's involvement in politics.
- It is not enough to just write down facts, no matter how correct they are. You must explain clearly how each fact caused an increase in women's involvement in politics.

Sources A and B are about the impact of the First World War on women in Scotland.

SOURCE A

Throughout the war, especially in Scotland, women worked hard for their communities. They had many different roles. Women worked as munitions workers or ran the voluntary hospitals. Some also led the many voluntary movements set up to help the war effort. By the end of the war, that had been fought in large part to maintain the rights of small countries, votes for women was an idea that was generally accepted.

SOURCE B

By 1916, it was clear that women had become a vital part of the war effort. One of these important war-related jobs was in munitions. In Scotland, the main munitions centres were in Glasgow, Clydebank and Gretna. Many other women used their nursing skills to help the wounded. By the end of the war, there were some gains for women. In political terms, many women could now vote.

2 Compare the views of Sources A and B about the impact of the war on women. (4 marks)

Success criteria

- You should interpret evidence from the sources.
- Make direct comparisons between the information in the sources.
- You can get up to 4 marks for making four simple comparisons between the information in the two sources.
- You can get up to 4 marks for making two developed comparisons between the information in the two sources.
- A simple comparison: 'Source A says … and Source B says …' will get 1 mark.
- A developed comparison: 'Sources A and B agree about the importance of women's war work. Source A says … and Source B says …' will get 2 marks.

9 What impact did the war have on politics in Scotland?

What is this chapter about?

In 1900, Scottish politics was dominated by the Liberals and Conservatives. However, the war caused big political changes. The Liberal Party went into long-term decline in Scotland. The Conservative Party (also known as the Unionist Party) increased its support. The new Labour Party gained confidence from being part of the wartime coalition and began to get more votes. Radical activity in the Clydeside area, things like strikes, demonstrations and protests, had always been just under the surface during the war and this was to come to a head in the 'Red Clydeside' events of early 1919.

By the end of this chapter you should be able to:

▸ Describe the effects the war had on Scotland's politics.
▸ Explain the events known as 'Red Clydeside'.

Politics in Scotland

The First World War destroyed support for the Liberal Party in Scotland. Before the war, the Liberals had been the dominant force but they were replaced by the Conservative Party, which grew in overall power and influence. At the same time, support for the new Labour Party was advancing. Evidence of the growth of socialism in Scotland was seen in the events of **Red Clydeside**.

Why did the Liberals lose support?

One reason for the collapse in support for the Liberals was the demands of the war. Liberals claimed to stand for freedom and choice but had introduced restrictions on many aspects of daily life. Conscription was one example. Some Liberals opposed the idea as it forced men into the army.

> **GLOSSARY**
> **Red Clydeside** a period of political unrest in Scotland in 1918–20

The war had also led to a split in the Liberals. In 1914, the party was united behind Asquith, its leader. However, in 1915 a coalition government was formed, which included some Conservative and Labour MPs. In 1916, Asquith was forced to resign as prime minister. Many politicians blamed him for the war not going well. He was replaced by Lloyd George. Supporters of Asquith left the government in protest and the party was divided between supporters of Lloyd George and Asquith. By the 1920s, the Liberal Party had ceased to be an effective political force.

Why did Conservative support grow after 1918?

The Conservatives (also known as Unionists or Tories) were seen as the party of patriotism and empire. In the post-war elections, many Conservative candidates were ex-army men.

The Conservatives' policies were aimed at middle-class voters. They tried to attract the new female voters by promising them help to support the family. They opposed the new idea of socialism. This appealed to voters who were frightened by the rise of the Labour Party. The middle class was also scared of **communism** as communists had seized control in a revolution in Russia. They were worried the same might happen in Scotland, especially when the Tory newspapers ran **scaremongering** stories of 'riots in George Square'.

The Conservative Party had many wealthy supporters so the party was well funded. This allowed it to maintain and develop its organisation across the country.

The Conservatives were also well led and used new methods like the cinema to put their ideas across. For many middle-class Scots, the Conservative Party was their natural home. Conservatives built up support in the rural areas of Scotland. They also appealed to young Scots who wanted to be successful in their lives. They claimed to represent traditional morals and values.

> **GLOSSARY**
>
> **Communism** a political movement wanting to create a classless society
>
> **Scaremongering** spreading frightening rumours
>
> **Constituency** an area which an MP represents in parliament

Why did the Labour Party grow in importance?

Before 1914, the Labour Party had no experience of government. The war changed this and in 1915 Labour was asked to join the coalition government. The government now listened to the trade unions and worked with them to run the economy more effectively.

Support for the party increased during the war. Before 1914, the Labour Party had never put up more than 78 candidates at election time. In 1918, it put up 361 candidates and won more than 2.25 million votes.

Party organisation also developed during the war. In 1914, there was no national organisation. By 1918, the Labour Party was well organised with separate **constituency** branches.

The question of whether to go to war or not had divided the Labour Party in 1914. Most members supported it but some did not. The end of the war saw the party reunite.

The war had led Labour to develop policies to deal with the post-war situation. These included a minimum wage and control of industry to help promote people's welfare.

The Labour Party also benefited from the growth in trade union membership, which stood at 4,135,000 in 1913. It increased to 6,533,333 by the end of the war.

What was Red Clydeside?

In 1917, there was a revolution in Russia which led to the country becoming a communist state. In simple terms, that meant that capitalists – wealthy people, landowners and businessmen who made money through their workers – lost their power and money.

At the same time, although Scottish workers were protesting about hunger and bad housing, they were mainly concerned about the changes to their working day forced on them by the wartime Defence of the Realm Act (DORA).

The government and property owners were afraid that Scottish workers would take the law into their own hands and possibly start a revolution in Scotland. It was easy to believe that revolution was not far away because the Russian revolution had also started with a few strikes in the main cities.

During and just after the end of the war, many workers in the Glasgow area were unhappy with changes to their jobs. In 1914, DORA made strikes illegal. The Munitions of War Act of 1915 was even stricter. With the introduction of conscription in 1916, skilled workers feared that they would be put under army control and sent to factories to do war work but with worse conditions and wage cuts.

What happened in Red Clydeside?

There was already tension in Glasgow in 1915 because of rent strikes and industrial strikes for better working conditions.

In early 1919, in Glasgow, the workers wanted the length of their working week reduced to 40 hours. They also demanded an increase in pay to £1 a day. A huge

> Above the heads of the workers, someone has flown a red flag. In small groups, read what the strike was about and how the authorities reacted. Now decide: if you could go back in time, would you have flown the red flag? What reasons do you have for your decision?

A famous photograph of the George Square meeting of strikers in January 1919. In those days communists were known as reds because they used a red-coloured flag. When a red flag flew in Glasgow, the government was afraid a revolution might be starting.

strike was called on 27 January 1919. Most workers in Glasgow supported this. When the strike ended on 31 January, a crowd met at George Square in Glasgow.

The government was extremely worried by these developments. There had been a revolution in Russia which had led to the collapse of the Russian Empire; the tsar and his family had been executed and civil war was raging across the land. The great fear in all countries was that this could spread to the rest of Europe. It was so important that the issue was discussed by the Cabinet, which approved a number of actions to be taken, including the possible deployment of troops, should this become absolutely necessary.

In the event, on the 31st of January, a riot broke out in George Square and the city council called for military assistance: 10,000 soldiers and six tanks arrived over the next three days. They spent three weeks guarding important points but were never needed. The strike ended a few days later with an agreement on working hours. However, the incident did much to establish the reputation of 'Red Clydeside' in the popular imagination.

Do a Google search to find out what happened to Shinwell and Hopkins for their role in Red Clydeside.

Newspapers reported that 90,000 people attended this demonstration and that running battles broke out between the police and strikers between George Square and Glasgow Green.

Emanuel Shinwell (left) and Harry Hopkins address the crowd in George Square from the front of the City Chambers on 'Bloody Friday', 31 January 1919

Why was Red Clydeside useful to the Tories in Scotland?

Communism was a big fear among the middle classes. Tory newspapers reported the communist revolution in Russia and the attempted revolution in Germany as the end of civilisation and declared that wealthy middle-class people would be murdered in their beds! Clearly, when riots broke out in Glasgow, the middle classes looked to the Tories to protect them.

In truth, there was no revolution in Glasgow. The military was not needed. Within a week of the riot, the workers had returned to work, agreeing to a 47-hour week.

Historian Trevor Royle has summed up the effects of Red Clydeside:

Even if Red Clydeside ultimately failed in revolution, the strikes and upheavals associated with its name still produced a major upheaval in Scotland's political history.

Activity 1

Summarise this chapter

Imagine that you are a newspaper journalist and that you have been asked to investigate and report on the political changes that have happened in Scotland as a result of the First World War.

Think about what sort of questions you might want answered. To help get you started, use the following hints:

▶ What sort of people supported each political party?
▶ What did each party stand for?
▶ What strengths/weaknesses did each party have?
▶ What effect did the change in the franchise have on each party?
▶ What effect did helping fight the war have on each party?

Write these questions down in your workbook or work file and add your own. Find evidence to answer these questions and note your answers in your workbook or work file.

Now you can plan your article. Make notes and structure what you are going to write in your report. Write your first draft of your article.

Read through your work carefully and mark any mistakes you spot with a green pen, then correct your work before handing it to your teacher.

Ensure that information which answers all the questions can be found in your article. Your article should be structured and well organised.

Activity 2

In your workbook or work file, write down the questions you would like answered about how the First World War changed politics in Scotland. You should try to think of at least three questions.

Dedicate a wall space for a 'No easy answers' board in the classroom. Hold a class discussion on whether your questions have been answered and agree on which questions should go on the classroom's 'No easy answers' board.

At various points during the course of the topic, revisit the ideas and questions on the board to see if your understanding has developed.

Question practice

National 4

Source A is by a modern historian about the changes in support for political parties as a result of the First World War.

SOURCE A

The Conservative Party gained a lot from the First World War. This was because people admired the strong support the Conservatives had shown for the war. Scots thought the Conservatives were very patriotic. The Conservatives were also well funded, often by people who were worried about the rise of Labour. The Labour Party did well out of the First World War as it had shown support for social issues such as housing, which were of great concern to Scots. Labour had shown support for the rent strikes.

Explain the reasons why the First World War changed people's support for political parties. You should use Source A and your own knowledge.

Success criteria

Include at least one piece of information explaining why the First World War changed people's support for political parties.

National 5

Explain why the First World War led to the decline of the Liberal Party in Scotland. (6 marks)

Here are some hints to get you started:

- divisions in the Liberal Party before the war
- divisions in the Liberal Party over the running of the war
- rivalry between Lloyd George and Asquith
- party splits in the 1918 election
- increasing support for both the Conservative Party and the Labour Party.

Success criteria

- You will need to write an introduction sentence that answers the question. For example, 'There are many reasons why the First World War led to the decline of the Liberal Party.'
- You must give six reasons or three developed points explaining why the First World War led to the decline of the Liberal Party.
- It is not enough just to write down facts, no matter how correct they are. You must explain clearly how each fact caused the decline of the Liberal Party.

10 To what extent had Scotland changed by 1928?

What is this chapter about?

By 1928, the world, and indeed Scotland, had changed as a result of the First World War. Scottish industry had not adapted and found it difficult to compete in both the British and world markets. The traditional industries of Scotland were in decline and this led to massive unemployment and workers' unrest. People wanted improvements to their working lives and living conditions and this brought about political and social changes that can still be seen today.

By the end of this chapter you should be able to:

▶ Describe the ways the economy of Scotland had changed between 1900 and 1928.
▶ Explain the problems that ordinary Scots faced by 1928.

What had happened to Scotland's industries?

The world which Scotland faced by 1928 was quite different from that of 1914.

Scotland's place within the empire had changed as a result of the war. Glasgow had lost its position as the 'second city of the empire'. Former markets were now competitors. The basic industries of Scotland were under pressure from the technologically advanced industries in the south of England, as well as in Canada and Australia. Emigration remained an escape route for Scots, the most popular destinations being Canada, Australia and South Africa. During the years 1921–31, over 550,000 people emigrated to what they hoped would be a better life.

New industrial centres, like Birmingham and Manchester, were more important now. The decline in Scotland's basic industries of shipbuilding, coal mining, and iron and steel making led to long-term unemployment for many workers. This led inevitably to industrial and social unrest.

The table below shows how much the shipbuilding industry had declined on Clydeside after the First World War.

Year	Number of workers
1920	100,000
1925	50,000
1929	10,000

Workers in Clydeside shipyards from 1920 to 1929

Workers tried to resist cuts to their wages, which led to unofficial strikes and protests. Those who were out of work found it very difficult to make ends meet.

Demobilised soldiers had expected to get their old jobs back, but this did not happen.

GLOSSARY

Demobilised taken out of active service

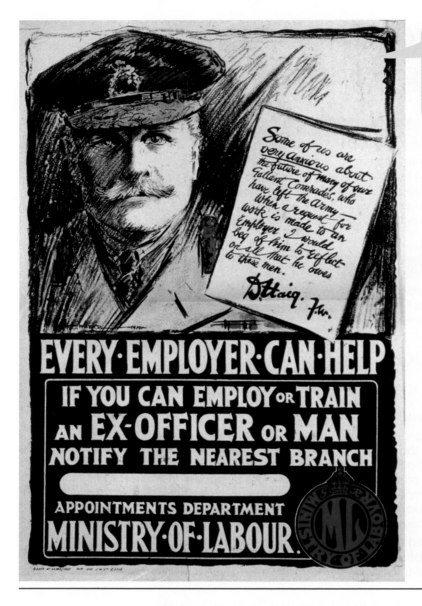

Poster asking employers to take on men who served during the First World War, featuring a personal plea from Field Marshal Douglas Haig

What was life like for Scotland's working class?

Many Scottish people still had poor health and bad housing conditions after the war. Government schemes lacked the money needed to make any real impact and people continued to live in single rooms with no proper water supplies or sanitation. 'Homes fit for heroes' became a hollow joke during this period.

However, for the four out of five Scots who did have a job, life did improve. New consumer industries created products that made workers' lives easier. Larger numbers of people could buy their own homes. There was more money which could be spent on leisure activities and other non-essential items. As a result, the quality of life for these people did improve.

There was a significant change in Scottish politics during and after the war. The success of the rent strikes and the Clyde Workers' Committee led the working classes to demand more from the government. In the 1920s, the government did try to improve housing in Scotland with **slum clearance** and council houses (now called social housing) for rent at fair prices.

GLOSSARY

Slum clearance demolishing unsuitable houses to make space for new homes

Compare the two photographs. List as many differences as you can between the pre-war housing in 1910 and the housing of the 1920s.

Slum housing in Glasgow in 1910 (top) and Mosspark housing estate in the 1920s (bottom)

What happened to Scottish politics?

The Liberal Party lost political support and the Conservative Party and the Labour Party became the two main parties within Scotland. This was reflected in the number of MPs elected in general elections.

Year	Liberals	Conservatives	Labour
1918	33	30	7
1922	27	13	29
1923	22	14	34
1924	8	36	26
1929	13	20	36

General election results for Scotland 1918–29

Draw a bar graph to show the varying successes of the political parties in Scotland in the 1920s.

Overall, the pride and the confidence which had existed before 1900 had disappeared by 1929. Many Scots looked back to what they saw as a 'golden era' and longed for a return to the 'good old days'.

Activity 1

Summarise this chapter

Work in pairs or small groups. Read through the information in this chapter and, in your workbook or work file, write down the different ways in which the First World War affected Scotland.

Get a large sheet of paper and draw jigsaw pieces. Write one fact in each piece and cut the pieces out. Divide the pieces equally among the group.

Each member of the group should research at least three pieces of information relating to the topic on each piece they have been given. This research should explain in greater depth how the First World War affected each topic. The new information should be added to the jigsaw pieces.

Reassemble the jigsaw into a poster. Be prepared to explain your information to the rest of the class. Hold a class discussion summarising the effects of the First World War on Scotland.

Activity 2

Debate

This activity is a 'walking debate'. Make four signs and put one in each corner of your classroom: 'Agree', 'Mostly Agree', 'Disagree' and 'Mostly Disagree'.

Create statements about the effects of the First World War on Scotland. The statements should evoke a range of responses. For example, 'Industry was badly affected by the First World War' is better than 'All industry was badly affected by the First World War'. Everyone should make up at least one additional statement.

Here are some statements to get you started:

▶ The scale of casualties badly impacted on Scottish society.
▶ Scottish women benefited from the war.
▶ Industry was badly affected by the First World War.
▶ Workers were dissatisfied after the First World War.
▶ The First World War led to many people emigrating.
▶ Many people supported Labour after the First World War.

Each statement is then read out and your classmates are allowed time to consider their opinion and a piece of information to support their opinion.

Each member of the class then moves to the corner which best describes how they feel about the statement. Be careful not to 'go along with the crowd', as there can be more than one response to these statements.

As you move, you should each take turns to explain why you are in that corner. If you switch your corner, be prepared to explain why. Each class member should explain their response to a statement at least once using detailed information to support their answer.

Hold a class discussion on whether the First World War was good or bad for Scotland overall.

Question practice

National 4

Source A is about how the First World War changed Scotland.

SOURCE A

The First World War changed Scotland in many ways. There was an overwhelming response to volunteering for the war. Scottish soldiers fought bravely, especially in the battles of 1915 and 1916. The Scottish home front made a big contribution to the war effort. There was a boom in industry and a strengthening of women's role in society because of the work they did during the war. Politics also changed. The Liberals lost support but others gained.

Explain in your own words the effect of the First World War on Scotland. You should use Source A.

Success criteria

Include at least one piece of information describing the effects of the First World War on Scotland.

National 5

How successful was the government in creating 'homes fit for heroes' after the First World War? (9 marks)

Planning your answer:

▶ In small groups or pairs, create a spidergram containing information on the positive and negative ways in which the First World War changed Scotland.

▶ Group the information into two paragraphs: 'Positive changes' and 'Negative changes'.

▶ Find connections between the different pieces of information and join them together. This will give you a structure for the order in which you talk about whether the First World War changed Scotland for the worse.

▶ Plan an overall response to the question.

▶ Show your plan to your teacher before starting your first draft.

▶ Read through your work carefully and mark any mistakes you spot with a green pen, then correct your work before handing it to your teacher.

▶ Rewrite the final draft of your answer.

Success criteria

▶ One mark is available for an introduction, which should contain background and factors that you are going to write about.

▶ One mark is available for balance in your answer. This means you will have to mention at least two factors discussing the impact of the First World War on Scotland. That means at least two paragraphs of writing.

▶ This sort of question does not have a factor in it. In paragraph one, you need to make sure you discuss the ways Scots gained from changes after the war. In the second paragraph, you should discuss the ways in which the First World War had a negative impact on Scots' lives.

▶ Five marks are available for the relevant and detailed knowledge points that you are going to explain in your answer.

▶ Two marks are available for your conclusion. One mark is given for a judgement and one mark is given for a supporting reason for your conclusion.

Glossary

A

Admiralty – the government department that ran the Royal Navy

Aliens – foreign-born people living in a country

Amalgamated – joined together

Artillery – heavy guns designed to destroy enemy positions

Attrition – wearing down the enemy

B

Barrage – long periods of gunfire

Battalion – part of an army

Big push – a major attack on the enemy

Black market – the illegal sale of things that should have been rationed

Blue on blue – soldiers killed or wounded accidentally by their own side

C

Capitalists – people who owned factories, businesses and transport and who ran these for private profit

Cavalry – soldiers on horseback

Censored – parts removed or cut out

Central Powers – a loose alliance of Germany, Austria–Hungary and Italy

Citation – special statement commending bravery

Communism – a political movement wanting to create a classless society

Condolence – expression of sympathy over a death

Conscription – compulsory military service

Constituency – an area which an MP represents in parliament

Cordite – explosive used in ammunition

Council houses – homes built by local authorities for local people to rent

Crofters – tenant farmers in the Highlands of Scotland

D

Demobilised – to be taken out of active service

Dilution – replacing skilled workmen with semi-skilled or unskilled workers

Diversify – change from making one product to others needed for the war effort

Dreadnought – a new class of super-battleship

Duck-boards – wooden planks placed along the base of a trench

E

Electorate – people who have the right to vote in an election

Empire – a group of nations under the control of a single ruling power

F

Fascines – bundles of wood used to fill in trenches

Franchise – the right to vote in public elections

H

Heavy industry – industries such as coal mining and steel making

L

Location factors – reasons why companies set up their businesses where they do

M

Martial – warlike

Martyr – a person who suffers or dies for what they believe

Militancy – aggressive or warring activity

N

Neutral – not taking sides

Non-combatant – a soldier who does not take part in the fighting

O

Outflank – to go round the side of the enemy

P

Pan-Slavism – a movement trying to bring about the unity of all Slav nations

Patriotism – love of one's country

Propaganda – information to influence public opinion

R

Realm – a country

Reconnaissance – spying on the enemy

Red Clydeside – a period of political unrest in Scotland in 1918–20

Reserved occupations – vital wartime jobs done by skilled men who could not be conscripted

S

Scaremongering – spreading frightening rumours

Shell shock – what is now called post-traumatic stress disorder

Slavic – a group of people found in central and eastern Europe

Slum clearance – demolishing unsuitable houses to make space for new homes

Slums – homes unfit for people to live in

Socialism – a political movement aiming to create an equal society

Stalemate – deadlock

Strikes – withdrawal of work to get employers to give in to workers' demands

Subsidies – financial help

Suffrage – right to vote

T

'Take the king's shilling' – to join the armed forces

Trade unions – associations representing particular groups of workers

Trench foot – an infection of the foot caused by standing in water for long periods of time

Triple Entente – a loose association of Britain, France and Russia

Z

Zero hour – the exact time an attack is launched

Index

A

Addison's Act (1919) 84
aeroplanes 41, 44–5
alcohol restrictions 49
Alien Registration Act (1914) 49
Alsace–Lorraine 13
Arras, Battle of 40
artillery 35, 36, 39, 40, 41
Asquith, Herbert 5, 76, 79, 89
Austria–Hungary 11, 18, 27, see also Central Powers

B

Balfour, Arthur 5
Balkans 11, 18–19
Barbour, Mary 82, 83
Belgium 22, 24, 26, 27, 42
black market 53
Bosnia 18–19
British Empire 2–3, 10
British Expeditionary Force (BEF) 26, 27

C

Cambrai, Battle of 43
Cat and Mouse Act (1913) 78–9
censorship 33, 49
Central Powers 13, 17
Chisholm, Mairi 54
Clyde Workers' Committee 97
coal mining 4, 63, 66
colonies: importance of 9–10
communism 90, 91, 93
conscientious objectors 55
conscription 55, 63, 89, 91
Conservative Party 5, 74, 89, 90, 98
Crawfurd, Helen 82, 83
Crofters' Holdings Act (1886) 6

D

Davison, Emily Wilding 76, 77
Defence of the Realm Act (DORA, 1914) 49, 91
demobilisation 95
Department of Scientific and Industrial Research 66
dilution scheme 52, 63
dogfights 44
dreadnoughts 14, 15
Drummond, Flora 75, 76
Dunlop, Marion Wallace 78

E

Eastern Front 27
economy 5, 62–6, see also industry
electricity 67
emigration 95
empires 2–3, 9–10
engineering 4, 63, 66
Europe, divisions in 17

F

Fairfield shipyard, Govan 63
farming 64, 66
Fawcett, Millicent 73, 79
Fisher, Admiral Sir John 14
fishing 4, 64
Fokker, Anton 44
Franz Ferdinand, Archduke, assassination of 9, 19

G

gas 38, 40, 42
George V, King 2, 76
Glasgow 4, 24, 82, 91–3, 95
Glasgow Women's Housing Association 82
Great War
    casualties 26, 27, 39, 40, 41, 56
    causes of 9–11, 13–15, 18, 19, 21
    land use 49
    notification of death 57
    opposition to 55
    Scottish volunteers 24–5, 26, 56

H

Haig, General Douglas 36–7, 39, 96
Highlands, unrest in 6
housing 6, 80–5, 96, 97, see also rent strikes
hunger strikes 78

I

Independent Labour Party (ILP) 5, 26, 55, 84, see also Labour Party
industrial unrest 5, 66, 91–2, 95
industry 4–5, 63–4, 66, 67, 95, 96
infantry 34, 39, 41
Inglis, Dr Elsie 53
iron industry 4, 63

J

jute industry 4, 64, 66

K

Kitchener, General Herbert 26

L

Labour Party 5, 74, 89, 90, 98, see also Independent Labour Party
Labour Representation Committee, see Labour Party
Liberal Party 89, 98
Lloyd George, David 49, 83, 84, 89
London, Treaty of 24
Loos, Battle of 38

M

machine guns 36, 37, 41, 44
Marne, Battle of 44
Men's League for Women's Suffrage 77
Military Service Acts 55
Ministry of Munitions 62, 63
munitions industry 51–2, 63

N

National Registrations Act 55
National Union of Women's Suffrage Societies (NUWSS) 73, 74
No Conscription Fellowship (NCF) 55
North British Locomotive Company 66
North British Rubber Company 63

P

Pan-Slavism 11
Pankhurst, Emmeline 75, 76
Passchendaele, Battle of 37
politics/political parties 5, 26, 55, 74, 84, 89, 90, 97, 98
population growth 6
propaganda 50

R

railways 41, 49, 62, 66
rationing 52–3
Red Clydeside 89, 91–3
Rent Restriction Act (1915) 83
rent strikes 81–3, 97
Representation of the People Act (1918) 80
reserved occupations 63
Russell, Bertrand 26
Russia 18, 22, 24, 27, 91, 92

S

Sarajevo, see Bosnia
Schlieffen Plan 22, 24, 26, 27
Scottish Churches League for Women's Suffrage 77
Scottish Federation of Women's Suffrage Societies 73
Scottish National War Memorial 58–9
Scottish Trade Unions 5
Scottish Women's Hospitals 53–4
shell shock 35
shipbuilding 4, 63, 65, 95
socialism 5, 55, 80, 89
Somme, Battle of the 37, 39
steel industry 4, 44, 63, 64
strikes 5, 66, 78, 81–3, 91–2, 95
suffrage 72–4, 80
suffragettes 75–7, 78
suffragists 73, 74, 75, 77

T

tanks 41, 43
textile industry 63, 64
Tirpitz, Admiral Alfred von 14
trade unions 5, 90
trench foot 34
trenches 27, 32–5
Triple Entente 17

U

unemployment 67, 95

W

Western Front 27, 32–45
    conduct of battles 35–7
    contribution of Scots 38–40
    trenches 27, 32–5
    war technology 41–5
Wheatley Housing Act (1924) 84
Wheatley, John 84
Wilhelm II, Kaiser 10, 24
women
    and action on housing 80–5
    legal rights 73
    and right to vote 72–80
    see also suffrage, suffragettes, suffragists
    opposition to war 83
    role of 51–4, 72–3
Women's Freedom League 76
Women's International League for Peace and Freedom 83
Women's Peace Crusade 83
Women's Social and Political Union (WSPU) 75–6

Y

Ypres 42